HALF-HEARTED ENEMIES

HALF-HEARTED ENEMIES

Nova Scotia, New England and the War of 1812

John Boileau

Formac Publishing Company Limited
Halifax

Copyright ©2005

Formac Publishing Company Limited acknowledges the support of the Cultural Affairs Section, Nova Scotia Department of Tourism, Culture and Heritage. We acknowledge the financial support of the Government of Canada through the Book Publishing Industry Development Program (BPIDP) for our publishing activities.
We acknowledge the support of the Canada Council for the Arts for our publishing program.

Canadian Cataloguing in Publication Data
Library and Archives Canada Cataloguing in Publication

Boileau, John
    Half-hearted enemies : Nova Scotia, New England and the War of 1812 / by John Boileau.

Includes bibliographical references and index.
ISBN 0-88780-657-0

    1. Nova Scotia—History—1784-1867. 2. New England—History—War of 1812.
3. Canada—History—War of 1812. 4. Nova Scotia—Relations—New England.
5. New England—Relations—Nova Scotia. I. Title.

FC2322.3.B65 2005   971.6'02   C2005-902336-8

Formac Publishing
Company Limited
5502 Atlantic Street
Halifax, Nova Scotia B3H 1G4
www.formac.ca

Distributed in the
United States by:
Casemate
2114 Darby Road, 2nd Floor
Havertown, PA 19083

Printed and bound in Canada

Table of Contents

ACKNOWLEDGEMENTS

Very few works of non-fiction are written in isolation; most of them draw, to one degree or another, on the efforts and research of many others. This book is no exception, and I am indebted to several writers and researchers who have studied various aspects of the War of 1812 previously. In particular, I must thank Dr. Brian Cuthbertson, whose extensive research and knowledge of Melville Island and its prisoners of war have been particularly invaluable to me. Brian possesses an unrivalled goldmine of information on this aspect of the war, all of which he willingly shared with me.

I must also acknowledge the contributions of my sister, Patricia Theriault, who spent countless hours driving around Maine, where she now lives, to visit not only state institutions, but also local museums and historical societies, conducting research for me on the British occupation of eastern Maine during the war. Pat is a thorough and indefatigable researcher.

The Cambridge Military Library, itself a fascinating product of that very occupation, remains a well-kept secret. A tranquil haven in the middle of a bustling city, it harks back to the days when Halifax was an isolated outpost of the Empire. As always, Librarian Jeanne Howell and Custodian Master Corporal Michaela Brister could not have been more helpful.

Although I had been thinking about a book on Nova Scotia and the War of 1812 for some time, it was the urging of Guy MacLean,

President of the Northwest Arm Heritage Association, that persuaded me to suggest the subject to my publisher. Guy and the members of his association were key players in preventing the loss of Deadman's Island, an important part of our history, to commercial development.

Thanks are due as well to Sandra McIntyre, Managing Editor at Nimbus Publishing Limited for permission to quote from *Diary of a Frenchman: François Lambert Bourneuf's Adventures from France to Acadia 1787–1871*, edited and translated by J. Alphonse Deveau and published in 1990.

I must also thank Publisher Jim Lorimer and Senior Editor Elizabeth Eve at Formac Publishing Company Limited for their cooperation in bringing this story to print. Also at Formac, Production Editor Martin Tooke and Copy Editor Jerry Lockett showed once again how essential editors are to the writing process.

Finally, I must mention my wife, Miriam, whose support on the home front ensures I actually get to write. I dedicate *Half-Hearted Enemies* to her.

To all these and others not specifically mentioned by name, I owe my thanks.

When dealing with the events of almost two centuries ago, it is often difficult to confirm exactly what happened. Facts conflict with one another, information is missing, national views distort events and the lives of the "invisible" people of the day—ordinary people—go unrecorded. While this can make it more difficult to tell the whole story, it is no excuse for not telling it.

J.B.B.

PREFACE

Although the War of 1812 has long since passed from human memory, it lives on in many ways across Nova Scotia. For the most part, the province was on the periphery of the war, far removed from the land battles along or near the international border at Detroit, the Niagara Peninsula, Crysler's Farm and Chateauguay, or the naval engagements on the Great Lakes and the open oceans. Nova Scotia was not invaded; no battles were fought here. Yet, the province was involved in the war, both directly and indirectly.

Warships of the Royal Navy stationed at Halifax sought combat with ships of the United States Navy and blockaded the American coast. Privateers sailed from Nova Scotia ports looking for lucrative prizes. Prisoners and black refugees were brought to Halifax. In addition, the two most successful invasions of the United States had a Nova Scotia involvement. One started in the province and produced lasting benefits to the colony. The other had its sad conclusion here. And throughout the war, provincial merchants, farmers, tradesmen and others made money by supplying or trans-shipping goods to both sides.

Most Nova Scotians found themselves in a dilemma: their country was at war with the United States, but it was a war they did not want. The ties between the tiny colony and the new republic, especially those with its close neighbour, New England, were exceptionally strong. Commercially, a flourishing trade existed between the two regions to the mutual benefit of Bluenosers and Yankees. Many Nova Scotians, or their parents or grandparents, had come from New England and had family and friends living there.

While the attitude of the province's Loyalists towards the United States was not particularly marked by warm feelings—they had fled the Revolution with few of their belongings—a surprising number of them maintained close commercial connections with their former home. Another group of American immigrants had come to Nova Scotia after the Expulsion of the Acadians in 1755. These largely New England Planters (the word meant "farmer" at the time), the so-called "Pre-Loyalists," occupied much of the land forcibly vacated by the Acadians. Most of them retained strong connections to the United States.

In fact, the ties were so solid that Nova Scotia even had its own small rebellion during the American Revolution, with the aim of making the province the Fourteenth Colony. George Washington, at the urging of rebels in the colony, actually con-sidered invading Nova Scotia. Fortunately, he decided against it and the revolt failed.

The events of the War of 1812 are remembered in many ways across Nova Scotia. Settlements, fortifications, monuments, graves, plaques, cannons, mementoes, celebrations, a ghost ship—even a university and a library—perpetuate its memory. They are daily reminders of the time when Nova Scotians and New Englanders were half-hearted enemies. This book tells the stories of Nova Scotia's part in that long-ago conflict.

J.B.B.

"Lindisfarne"

Glen Margaret, Nova Scotia

New Year's Day, 2005

INTRODUCTION
"A MERE MATTER OF MARCHING"

If there ever was a pointless war, the War of 1812 was certainly it. In the words of maritime historian Faye Kert, it "seems to have been declared by the unprepared and fought by the unwilling for reasons that remain unexplained." The war was fought between the United States and Great Britain, and Canada was the main battleground.

The war was a long time coming. Ever since the Americans won their hard-fought independence in 1783, relations with Great Britain had generally not been good. In particular, the high-handed attitude of the British, who tended to look down on the Americans as crude and rude upstarts and not as the citizens of a real country, did not help.

"FREE TRADE AND SAILORS' RIGHTS" was hardly a motto to stir the soul to mortal combat, smacking as it does of commercial overtones, but these two related themes formed the basis for America's grievances against Britain, complaints that would see the world's two most powerful English-speaking nations go to war for the second time in 30 years.

By 1812, Britain had long been at war with France. That conflict started in a spate of revolutionary fervour, with Louis XVI of France losing his head to the guillotine at the hands of his countrymen on January 21, 1793. When Britain sent the French ambassador packing, France, already fighting Austria, Piedmont and Prussia, promptly declared war on Britain, the Netherlands and Spain in response. Almost a quarter of a century of continuous warfare on land and sea followed.

It only ended on June 18, 1815, 12 miles south of the Belgian capital of Brussels, near the little village of Waterloo, when the Duke of Wellington decisively defeated Napoleon Bonaparte and ended his dreams of French global domination. However, before Napoleon's defeat, the conflict between Britain and France indirectly led to other hostilities, culminating in the War of 1812 between the United States and Great Britain—a war often referred to as the "Second American War of Independence."

Initially the United States remained neutral in the war between Britain and France, despite the considerable naval and military assistance France had rendered to the Americans during their earlier War of Independence. The new republic had soon become one of the world's major shipping nations and depended upon trade with both sides for much of her revenue. Unfortunately, her commerce suffered at the hands of both the British and French as they enforced their blockades against one another. To Britain, nothing else mattered besides winning the war against France. If she trampled the feelings—or the rights—of some neutral nations in the achievement of that aim, it was of little consequence.

As the chief neutral nation trading with the French, the United States would inevitably find herself confronting the might of British sea power. In November 1807, Britain passed Orders-in-Council, establishing a blockade of Napoleon's Europe and forbidding any nation to trade with the enemy. This regulation affected American shipping the most.

To make matters worse, Britain frequently resorted to forcibly impressing seamen to serve in the Royal Navy, including citizens of other nations, especially the United States. In the Americans' case, the British claimed "inalienable allegiance," or the inability of people to change their citizenship without the approval of their country of birth. This meant that every American over 30 years of age remained a British subject. The Americans rejected this idea outright. Much to their outrage, impressment into the Royal Navy happened not only on the high seas, but also in American territorial waters. Over time, the Royal Navy pressed thousands of American seamen.

Life on British warships was challenging and brutal. British sailors frequently deserted, and the preferred place to desert was the United States. The desertion of four Royal Navy seamen led to the first armed clash between Britain and the United States since the American Revolution. These four runaway sailors later served on an American frigate, *Chesapeake* (38 guns), where they were known to be deserters but were assumed to be American citizens. In fact, three of them were Americans, but all had received a bounty to join the Royal Navy.

When American authorities refused all British diplomatic requests to return them, Vice Admiral George Cranfield Berkeley, the Commander-in-Chief at Halifax, ordered several of his captains to stop and search the *Chesapeake* for deserters if they encountered her outside the limits of the United States.

Chesapeake proceeded to sea from Hampton Roads on June 22, 1807, under Commodore John Barron. She passed British ships blockading the entrance. They were waiting outside American territorial waters for the departure of two French ships undergoing repairs at Annapolis. When an officer from one of the British ships, *Leopard* (50 guns), boarded *Chesapeake*, Barron denied having any British deserters on board and refused to be searched. *Leopard*'s captain fired a shot across *Chesapeake*'s bows, which did not change Barron's mind, so he followed with three broadsides, killing three men and wounding eighteen, including her captain. A British boarding party subsequently discovered the four deserters and sent them to Halifax for trial. The court found them guilty and sentenced one to death and each of the others to 500 lashes. The death sentence was carried out by hanging, but Berkeley pardoned the others and spared them the lash.

The *"Leopard–Chesapeake* Affair" caused universal antipathy for Great Britain within the United States and led to American threats of war. The incident generated considerable diplomatic correspondence until finally settled five years later, in July 1812. The British returned the two remaining deserters, the third having died in prison. Despite the hatred and sense of humiliation that the incident stirred among Americans, particularly naval officers, it was not one of the stated reasons for going to war. Perhaps the United States felt it obtained the revenge it sought with the *Little Belt* incident.

In May 1811, Commodore John Rodgers in frigate *President* (44 guns) sighted a small British sloop-of-war, *Little Belt* (18 guns), off the American coast and chased her, probably to confirm her identity. When he caught up with her, it was dark and a shot rang out. An investigation never determined who fired first, and both sides accused the other. It really didn't matter; the United States Navy wanted to avenge *Chesapeake* and sought any excuse. A short, violent engagement followed. When it was over, *Little Belt* was badly shot up, with 11 men killed and 21 wounded. The possibility of war between the United States and Great Britain moved closer to reality.

The Orders-in-Council, impressment, blockade and violation of American territorial waters were all instrumental in leading the United States to war. These grievances were coupled with another long-standing problem between the two countries—suspicion and mistrust—a legacy from the Revolutionary War. This mistrust centred on Britain's continuing support for the native peoples, whose lands the Americans wanted for westward expansion, and non-settlement of outstanding Loyalist claims by the United States. At the same time, in what Americans would eventually come to call their "Manifest Destiny," the United States regarded the conquest of Canada as a legitimate goal.

The British simply could not believe the United States would go to war for the principles of free trade and freedom from her citizens being forced to serve in the Royal Navy. But by the spring of 1812, many Americans—the so-called "War Hawks"—did want war with Britain. The War Hawks were expansionists, primarily young Southerners and Westerners elected to Congress in 1810, whose territorial ambitions caused them to agitate for war with Britain. Consequently, support for war was strongest in the South, which was dependent on trade with France, and the West, which was enviously eyeing land in Upper Canada and in what was historically known as Indian Territory. It was weakest in Federalist New England, most affected by the embargo but still carrying on an active trade with the Maritimes, to the mutual benefit of both sides. New England farmers and merchants were supplying the British forces fighting Napoleon—many of them getting rich in the process—and did not want a war. They talked of secession and of making a separate peace with Britain. Some states even refused to supply their military quotas. Would James Madison, the scholarly fourth U.S. President, risk the cohesion of his young and fragile federation of states over matters of principle? Indeed he would.

American frustration came to a head in June with Madison's War Message to Congress. He charged Britain with "a series of acts, hostile to the United States as an independent and neutral nation." He outlined his nation's grievances and declared war. Ironically, the British Government repealed the Orders-in-Council on June 16, two days before the American declaration, but when the news reached Madison, it did not change his mind.

Thomas Jefferson, President before Madison, had sadly neglected the small United States Navy and regular army, partly as a cost-saving measure, but also because he was a pacifist and did not see war as either a means or an end. In any case, most people believed that the militia—in effect, each state's private army—could stand up to British regulars, a popular misconception dating from the Revolution.

The militia had a number of drawbacks. No militiaman was required to serve the United States for more than three months in any one year. A number of states had laws forbidding them to be employed outside the borders of their home state without the militiamen's permission, and that of their governor. The New England governors pointedly refused to allow their militia to do this, much to the despair of the President and the War Hawks.

When Madison finally declared war on June 18, 1812, the Americans believed there would be little opposition from Canada, or British North America as it was then called. Its garrisons were undermanned, given that Britain had sent most of its soldiers to fight Napoleon in Spain. An open border almost 1,800 miles long was defended by only 4,000 British regulars, supported by another 3,000 Canadian militiamen. Seven and a half million Americans expected that the conquest of half a million Canadians would be, in Jefferson's words, "a mere matter of marching." The Americans were in for a surprise.

Most of the fighting took place along the international border in Upper and Lower Canada, on the Great Lakes and on the Atlantic Ocean. The first two years of the war saw a number of cross border skirmishes, one in Lower Canada and the rest in Upper Canada.

The war went badly for the Americans right from the start. Major General Sir Isaac Brock, the Administrator of Upper Canada, anticipated American advances in the west and launched successful attacks against Michilimackinac and Detroit in mid-July. His brilliant pre-emptive strikes immediately put the Americans on the defensive and caused them to abort their three-pronged invasion plans. The Battle of Queenston Heights followed in October. It was another British victory, although it resulted in the death of Brock. After a further British success at Frenchtown in January 1813, military operations ceased for the winter.

In 1813, the Americans intended to seize Kingston with the aim of cutting the link between the Canadas, but they opened their campaign by attacking York (now Toronto), the capital of Upper Canada, in April. They occupied the town for a few days, burning public buildings and taking naval stores. In May, American forces captured Fort George at the mouth of the Niagara River, but not before the British garrison had escaped. The withdrawing troops turned on their American pursuers and defeated them at the towns of Stoney Creek and Beaver Dams, taking many prisoners in the process and driving them back into the fort, where they remained until December. When they departed, the Americans burned Newark (now Niagara-on-the-Lake). The burning of York and Newark were acts the Americans would come to regret, as later in the war their own capital at Washington was occupied and burned in retaliation.

Further west, the Americans succeeded in defeating a British force at Moraviantown on the Thames River in October. The battle also resulted in the death of Tecumseh, a native leader and major ally of the British. Other battles on land that year saw British successes against a two-pronged American attempt to take Montreal, at Chateauguay and Crysler's Farm, as well as the capture of Fort Niagara on the American side of the river and the burning of Buffalo. The 1814 campaign season opened in early July with an invasion of Canada, when an American force crossed the Niagara River, seized Fort Erie and defeated the British at Chippewa shortly afterward. Lundy's Lane followed at the end of the month, a bitter contest fought by exhausted troops in the middle of the night. It ended in a draw. The Americans abandoned Fort Erie on November 5, and never attempted to invade Canada again.

When the war against Napoleon in Europe drew to a close, the British were finally able to free up sufficient troops to attack the United States. Invasions followed at Lake Champlain, the Chesapeake Bay area and eastern Maine in August, and at New Orleans in January 1815. For the British, the first resulted in a withdrawal, the second in a partial victory, the third in a complete victory and the last in an utter defeat.

British Governor-in-Chief Sir George Prevost, a former lieutenant-governor of Nova Scotia, aborted his attack at Plattsburg after the defeat of his supporting naval force on Lake Champlain. When word reached the peace negotiators in the Belgian city of Ghent, it forced the British to lower their demands. The British defeat at New Orleans, coming as it did after the peace treaty had already been signed but before the news arrived in North America, had no effect on the war's outcome.

Several naval battles were fought on the Great Lakes. Neither side established a clear supremacy over the other on Lake Ontario, but the Americans gained control of Lake Erie in September 1813. At sea, it was a different story. Much to the surprise of the British, the growing expertise of the fledgling United States Navy bested the Royal Navy on many occasions. One big exception to the string of American naval victories was the capture of *Chesapeake* by *Shannon* off Boston on June 1, 1813.

Like their practical New England neighbours, the equally prag-
matic Nova Scotians had no appetite for war. They were fearful of
the disruption it would cause to the lucrative seaborne trade
involving both regions. Nova Scotia Lieutenant-Governor Sir John
Coape Sherbrooke essentially established a truce with the New
Englanders within days of the American declaration of war.
Sherbrooke had been appointed lieutenant-governor in 1811,
when he was 47 years old. A capable British Army officer, he had
previously served in Nova Scotia in 1784–85, and then in the
Netherlands, India and the Mediterranean. Under Wellington in
Spain he distinguished himself against Napoleon. During his time
in India, he began to experience recurring illness and by the time
he came to Nova Scotia he was in poor health. This deterred neither his military zeal nor his competence.

On July 3, 1812, Sherbrooke issued a proclamation to the residents of Nova Scotia and New Brunswick, his concerns for the
interests of merchants and traders clearly manifesting themselves.
In it, he stated that no good could come from predatory warfare
against the defenceless residents living on the shores of the United
States that bordered the two provinces.

On the advice of His Majesty's Council—the executive body that
governed Nova Scotia, with many of its members drawn from the
mercantile elite—he ordered all the King's subjects under his control to abstain from molesting those residents. In addition, they
were on no account to interfere with unarmed American vessels
engaged in the peaceful pursuit of trade as long as the Americans
acted in the same way towards them.

The next day, Sherbrooke notified Britain of a shortage of provisions in the colony and advised that the only source of supply was
the United States. He followed this a month later with information
that the Americans wanted British goods from Nova Scotia. On
October 13, 1812, the British issued an Order-in-Council authorizing Halifax, as well as Saint John and St. Andrews in New Brunswick,
to trade certain specified articles with any American port, using only
American or neutral trading vessels as means of transport.
Consequently, while a state of war existed between Great Britain and

the United States and battles were being fought in the Canadas, Nova Scotians at first remained generally removed from the war.

Both Nova Scotians and New Englanders wanted to ensure that trade between them continued. The canny merchants of Nova Scotia and New England knew there was money to be made during wartime. Under a system of trading licences that sprang up immediately after the United States declared war— plus a little circumvention of the law here and there—Nova Scotia and New England merrily sold goods to each other and to the Americans and British fighting it out in land and sea battles far away.

With these licences, New England ships could enter Halifax or Saint John harbours at any time, safe in the knowledge they would be unharmed. Occasionally, Yankee merchants would arrange to have their ships seized by the British and taken to these ports where, under the pretence of ransoming their vessels, the owners were paid for their cargoes. The system kept both sides happy, at least for the time being.

In fact, if it had not been for American provisions, the British would have had great difficulty in prosecuting the wars against France and America. These provisions were shipped through Halifax to Wellington's army in Spain and Portugal, to British soldiers in the Canadas, to Newfoundland and to Nova Scotia itself for the civilian population and the Royal Navy. American merchants even ended up supplying the ever-growing British fleet that blockaded their own coasts and reduced many of their new capital city's public buildings to ashes.

In the same way, British goods from the United Kingdom, Ireland and the British West Indies were wanted—and needed— in the United States. For nearly three years, Nova Scotia served as a clearinghouse for much of North America's commerce, modifying traditional trade routes in the process.

Besides contributing to Nova Scotia's prosperity, this licenced trade had another important benefit, one Sherbrooke valued more highly than the trade itself. A year after the war started, he wrote to Lord Bathurst, Secretary for War and the Colonies, informing him

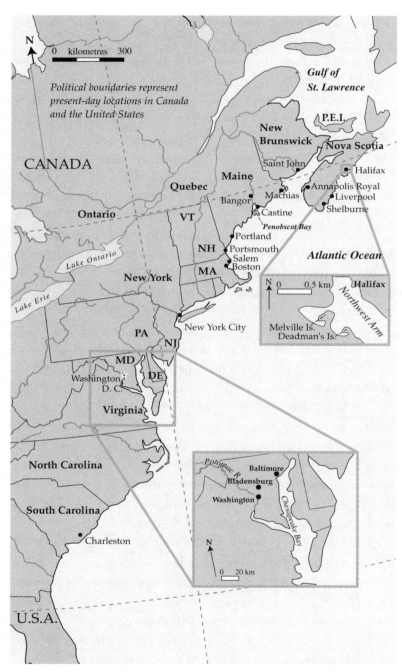

Nova Scotia's involvement in the War of 1812 ranged along the eastern seaboard of North America.

that the great amount of business with the United States had brought an unexpected advantage to the province.

He observed that the people of New England were now engaged in more trade and were doing so more eagerly than before. He thought the advantages brought by this licenced commerce drew their attention away from the war. If trade had been closed to the New Englanders, their "hostile energies" would have been directed against the British North American colonies. In the end, Sherbrooke estimated that licenced dealings had helped the region's security more than an additional force of several thousand men.

What Sherbrooke saw as an advantage meant little to the merchants, who were growing rich on the lucrative trade in provisions for the army and navy. Although the list of items allowed for exportation to the United States grew during the war—eventually it even included prize goods taken from the American ships—the blockading ships of the Royal Navy tended to rigidly enforce the British navigation laws. These laws were a form of trade protectionism designed to restrict portions of Britain's shipping trade to British-owned vessels only. They were finally repealed in the mid-nineteenth century.

The British, using the fleet based at Halifax under Vice Admiral Herbert Sawyer, did not begin a blockade of the American coast as soon as the war broke out. They had hoped a lack of warlike actions on their part, including the cancellation of the Orders-in-Council, would convince the Americans to reconsider their decision to declare war. When it became obvious Madison was not going to change his mind, the British ordered Vice Admiral Sir John Borlase Warren, who replaced Sawyer shortly after the war began, to blockade the American coast, which he did in February 1813.

Warren initially confined his blockade to Chesapeake Bay and the Delaware River, as the British wanted to make the southern states, who most strongly supported the war, feel its effects.

In the Chesapeake area, the British did not limit themselves to simply stopping shipping, but also conducted raids inland with landing parties of soldiers and marines, to cut off American supplies and destroy their foundries, stores and public works. The

Vice Admiral Sir John Borlase Warren

majority of the British fleet left the Chesapeake Bay area in September 1813 to winter in Halifax, leaving behind a few ships to maintain the blockade, which was soon extended northward to cover Long Island Sound. The British fleet returned to the Chesapeake in early 1814, determined that this year's campaign would be more effective than the previous one.

Vice Admiral Sir Alexander Cochrane, age 39, replaced Warren as naval Commander-in-Chief in March. Cochrane was given responsibility for the entire Atlantic and Gulf coasts of the United States. A Revolutionary War veteran, he arrived with a desire to give the Americans "a complete drubbing before peace is made." He expressed the hope of circumscribing their northern limits and gaining command of the Mississippi River. Shortly after issuing this proclamation, with ships and men freed up by the cessation of the war in Europe, Cochrane extended the blockade northwards, to the New Brunswick border.

British warships, many of them from Halifax, blockading the United States, turned away merchant vessels carrying items not on the approved list. When Nova Scotian merchants protested, the

British government refused to intervene, saying it was Cochrane's decision as the commander on the spot. The British government pointed out that authorizing British subjects to trade with the enemy while the American coast was blockaded would unfairly bar neutral countries from engaging in trade while one of the warring parties was doing so.

Both Bluenose and Yankee ingenuity would get around these restrictions later in the war when a brisk trade across the new "border" at Castine was established during the British occupation of eastern Maine.

Merchants, farmers, fishermen and tradesmen all made money from contracts with the large British fleet and army stationed in Nova Scotia. Businessmen and government officials lavishly entertained British naval and army officers. Several shareholders of privateering vessels, like Enos Collins, made personal fortunes from auctioning off the cargoes of their captured prizes as well as the prize ships themselves.

One company to benefit from the war was the firm of A. Cunard and Son. In 1780, during the American Revolution, the Cunard family, their prosperous merchant fleet confiscated by the Americans, had fled north with thousands of other Loyalists. Abraham Cunard, a skilled carpenter, settled in Halifax and worked in the Royal Navy dockyard as a foreman artificer while improving his ten-acre land grant, which ran from Brunswick Street down to the harbour.

He slowly expanded his carpentry business and eventually acquired a ship in 1808. He bought his second ship—a privateer's prize—in partnership with his son, Samuel. As a result of being issued one of the first licences for trading with the Americans, the Cunard shipping business grew rapidly and prospered during the war. With its third ship—another prize—the company started carrying transatlantic passengers in 1813. Cunard's Wharf became one of the city's busiest as father and son oversaw the building and repairs of ships.

In the last year of the war, Abraham turned the business over to his son and changed its name to S. Cunard and Company. In a few years, the Cunard fleet grew to be the largest in the north Atlantic, and pioneered the use of steamships.

As Halifax reached its peak of prosperity, the seedier side of wartime life revealed itself. Sailors and soldiers reeled about the city's streets in a drunken stupor at all times of night and day. Although Halifax historian Thomas Akins was only a small boy during the war, he recorded the first-hand accounts of others:

> *The upper streets were full of brothels; grog-shops and dancing houses were to be seen in almost every part of town. A portion of Grafton Street was known under the appellation of Hogg Street from a house of ill-fame kept by a person of that name. The upper street along the base of Citadel Hill between the north and south barracks was known as "Knock Him Down Street"* [Brunswick Street], *in consequence of the number of affrays and even murders committed there. No person of any character ventured to reside there, nearly all the buildings being occupied as brothels for the soldiers and sailors. The streets of this part of town presented continually the disgusting sight of aban-doned females of the lowest class in a state of drunken-ness, bare headed, without shoes, and in the most filthy and abominable condition.*

These and other areas, such as the "Beach" (Lower Water Street), co-existed with the splendid mansions of nearby Argyle and Barrington Streets. Without running water, the streets became a disgusting mess. Townsfolk emptied slops directly into the gutters, to collect in foul-smelling puddles. Outhouses and cesspits, neglected in the poorer parts of town, overflowed into the same pools. Fighting between the navy's press gangs and the townsmen was a common occurrence, but it almost went unnoticed in the continuous hubbub.

Yet, despite the city's prosperity, that great leveller, smallpox, struck during the winter of 1814–15, and hundreds of civilians and military personnel perished, regardless of whether they were rich or poor.

Even long before the War of 1812 began, the seemingly interminable war with Napoleon had brought prosperity to Nova Scotia from military and naval contracts as well as French prizes. The war with the United States added to the province's wealth. Nova Scotia historian Beamish Murdoch lived through the war as a teenager, and captured the spirit of the era:

> *The effects of the war upon this province, and particularly upon the people of Halifax, were very marked. Always sympathizing closely with the national glory of Great Britain, they were now drawn more than ever to feel a lively interest in military and naval transactions. The operations of the combatants were brought much more near than ever, and on the sea were more frequent. Our harbour had become the temporary home of the ships of war, and the place where their prizes were brought and disposed of. Our youths were eager to participate in the path that seemed to lead, by a few short steps, to honour, glory and fortune . . . . The little capital, then occupying a restricted space, became crowded. Trade was active. Prices rose. The fleet increasing, provisions were in great demand, and this acted as a large bounty in favour of the agriculturalist and the fisherman. Rents of houses and buildings in the town were doubled and trebled. A constant bustle existed in our chief streets. Cannon were forever noisy. It was the salute of a man-of-war entering or leaving, practicing with the guns, or celebrating something or somebody.*

An indication of the growing trade is shown in the revenue receipts for the port of Halifax during the war. They tripled, from £31,041 in the first year of the war to £93,759 in the last year. In 1815, they were still double those of 1812, probably due in part to the late arrival of the news of the signing of the peace treaty, which did not reach Nova Scotia until March 1815.

For many Nova Scotians, at least initially, it was as if there never was a war on. Most people were quite content to let it stay that way.

But the fact of war was soon driven home once the news of several Royal Navy defeats reached the province and privateers began bringing their captured prizes into port. The hope that Nova Scotia would not be involved soon faded, and the province became a key component in the war as a naval and military base, provider and trans-shipment point for war supplies, source of privateers, site of a penal complex for prisoners of war and refuge for escaped slaves.

In the end, the War of 1812 resolved none of the issues over which it was fought. Once it was over, both sides went back to the *status quo* that prevailed before the war. In this sense, it was a pointless war and never should have occurred. Perhaps the attitudes of the "half-hearted enemies" of Nova Scotia and New England were the right ones after all.

1

"DON'T GIVE UP THE SHIP!"

In 1812, Britain possessed the most powerful navy the world had ever known. Hundreds of warships were in commission, a result of the long, drawn-out war with Revolutionary France, which was sparked by the beheading of Louis XVI in 1793. At the same time, the French Navy was in a sorry state, after years of neglect. The Royal Navy's growing fleet bested the French on several occasions in the sea battles that followed the outbreak of war, even though many of its ships were undermanned. Some of these encounters would become the most famous naval actions in history.

In mid-1794, in a four-day running battle known ever since as the Glorious First of June, two equal-sized squadrons clashed 400 miles off the French coast. The British captured six French ships and sank a seventh.

Spain joined France in the war against Britain in 1796, threatening the Royal Navy in the Mediterranean. The next year, a large, but relatively untrained, Spanish fleet sailed from the Mediterranean, intending to join French ships off Brest for an invasion of England. A British fleet met the Spanish ships off Cape St. Vincent. The Spanish might have avoided a confrontation but for the intervention of a young British captain, Horatio Nelson. Nelson prevented the escape of part of the fleet as well as capturing two Spanish vessels.

In 1798, France decided to occupy Egypt at the urging of Napoleon Bonaparte, who was recognized as a tactical and strategic genius. Nelson, now an admiral, commanded 13 British ships sent to counter the French invasion. On August 1, he surprised the French squadron, also comprising 13 ships, at anchor, when some of the French crews were ashore. By the time the Battle of the Nile was over, only two French ships had escaped. Britain now dominated the oceans: few French ships dared to challenge the Royal Navy.

On November 9, 1799, Napoleon became First Consul of France, in effect the country's dictator. The Royal Navy now concentrated its efforts on blockading France and her allies and providing convoy escorts. Then, on March 27, 1802, the Treaty of Amiens between Britain and France brought peace to the continent for the first time in a decade, but the respite was short-lived. Hostilities recommenced in May 1803. Over the next two years the Royal Navy continued both to frustrate Napoleon's planned invasion of Britain, and to block French challenges in the Mediterranean, the Indian Ocean and the Caribbean. During this time, Napoleon became Emperor of the French.

The final French defeat at sea came in 1805, again at Nelson's hand. A French fleet under Admiral Pierre Villeneuve broke through Nelson's blockade of Toulon and escaped into the Atlantic, where it was joined by Spanish ships. The combined fleet sailed to the West Indies, 20 ships pursued by Nelson's 10, then back to Europe. On October 21, Nelson's fleet, now 27-strong, met Villeneuve's, now reinforced to 33, off Spain's Cape Trafalgar, near Cadiz. In the five-hour battle that followed, the British captured 18 French and Spanish ships, and the remainder fled. At his moment of triumph, Nelson was fatally wounded by a sharpshooter as his flagship, *Victory*, engaged in close combat with a French ship.

Nelson's genius had conclusively destroyed French naval power. Trafalgar remains the most decisive naval victory in history, but although it firmly established Britain as master of the seas, the Royal Navy would soon discover that it was not invincible.

As far as the British were concerned, by 1812 the Royal Navy's warships had protected not only Britain, but also the rest of the world—including the United States—from Napoleon's ambitions for almost 20 years. In the words of American naval strategist Admiral Alfred Mahan: "Those far distant, storm-beaten ships, upon which the Grand Alliance [Napoleon's coalition] never looked, stood between it and the domination of the world."

Despite the growing warlike behaviour and threats from America over various maritime issues, few in Britain believed the United States would actually declare war. President Thomas Jefferson had misguidedly neglected the U.S. Navy, a policy his successor, James Madison, continued. The Americans possessed only 16 fighting ships, plus some 62 small gunboats—useless in open water and not much better inshore—built under Jefferson partly as a cost-saving measure and partly because of his opposition to standing armies and navies. It seemed outside the realm of reason that a few American warships could challenge the proven, overwhelming might of the Royal Navy, the navy of Nelson. Yet, in the space of a few months, that is exactly what happened. In a series of five unprecedented single-ship actions, American vessels bested the British.

Although Halifax's North American Squadron was now larger than at any time since the start of the war with France in 1793, it was significantly smaller than it had been during the American Revolution. In June 1812, the squadron's 20 largest warships included Vice Admiral Herbert Sawyer's flagship *Africa* (60 guns) and the frigates *Guerrière* (38 guns), *Shannon* (38 guns), *Belvidera* (36 guns) and *Aeolus* (32 guns). There were also six gun-sloops, two gun-brigs and seven or eight small schooners. Part of the problem lay with the British Admiralty, and Nova Scotia even commissioned the private armed sloop *Gleaner*, a captured American privateer, for provincial service to help make up for navy shortfalls.

The squadron grew throughout the war and kept Nova Scotia safe from invasion. By the end of the conflict, it had captured 12 American warships and burned three others, against a loss of six of its own vessels. In addition, it brought nearly 500 captured American merchant ships as prizes into Halifax—almost three-quarters of the total seized—and burned at least another

200 vessels. It also captured 92 of the 93 privateers adjudicated by the court.

The Halifax squadron's blockade of the American coast bottled up all but one warship and had a tremendous impact on American merchant shipping, while its convoy escorts protected British commerce. Yet, numbers alone do not decide naval supremacy.

America's main strength lay in three 44-gun super-frigates: *United States*, *Constitution* and *President*, as strong as British ships of the line and faster than any British 38-gun vessels. Other warships included the frigates *Chesapeake* (38 guns), *Constellation* (38 guns), *Congress* (38 guns), *Essex* (32 guns) and *Adams* (28 guns), plus four gun-sloops and four little gun-brigs. Initially, apart from a few of the largest vessels, no British warships were a match for the new American heavy frigates. This fact would be driven home in the most dramatic way in a very short space of time once the war started.

When Madison declared war, several American ships were undergoing refit or repair, while another half dozen were at sea. The remainder, *United States*, *President*, *Congress*, *Hornet* and *Argus*, were in harbour at New York, ready for sea, under the command of Commodore John Rodgers.

On June 21, Rodgers sailed in search of a large British convoy he knew had departed Jamaica on May 20. As his squadron sailed north, Rodgers ran into Captain Richard Byron in the frigate *Belvidera* on June 23. He gave chase. His own ship, *President*, got within range and sent a few 24-pound rounds crashing into *Belvidera*. Damaged, with dead and wounded seamen aboard, and still unaware of the declaration of war, the British frigate escaped to Halifax where Byron gave the alarm. He even managed to capture three prizes on the way.

Sawyer immediately formed a squadron under Philip Broke of *Shannon*, senior captain at Halifax. His orders to Broke were simple: "Find Rodgers and destroy him." The 35-year-old Broke had been waiting for years for just such an opportunity, his first independent command.

Broke set sail on July 5 for American waters in the company of the flagship *Africa* and the frigates *Guerrière*, *Belvidera* and *Aeolus*.

His squadron arrived off New Jersey in mid-July and began looking for Rodgers. On the afternoon of July 17, Broke's squadron sighted an American super-frigate off the coast. She was *Constitution* under Captain Isaac Hull, possibly the best combination of ship and commander in the United States Navy, having just put to sea intending to join Rodgers.

Constitution ran off before the British squadron. After a 48-hour chase, Hull managed to outrun his pursuers, leaving them humbled behind him. For the next three weeks, Broke's ships escorted a homeward-bound convoy out into the Atlantic. Then, with convoy duty finished, Broke ordered Captain James Dacres of *Guerrière* to sail independently for Halifax for an overdue refit, while he returned to the American coast. Meanwhile, Hull, who had put in at Boston, slipped out of the harbour and headed north in search of British ships. The Royal Navy's comeuppance was about to begin.

At about 2 pm on August 19, 1812, Hull encountered Dacres making his way towards Halifax at a position some 300 miles southeast of Sable Island. Under Dacres, a brash young captain, *Guerrière* may have looked good, but ship and captain were no match for *Constitution*. While new paint and shiny brass covered a multitude of sins, Dacres neither cared properly for his guns nor drilled his crew in gunnery. Perhaps he regarded victory as a right, and one not requiring any preparation to achieve.

Even without her defects, *Guerrière* was no match for *Constitution*. Hull's ship had the advantage in length, beam, number and size of guns, weight of shot, tonnage, crew size and the all-important standard of gunnery. Dacres, blissfully unaware of the odds against him, bravely—or perhaps arrogantly—stood to meet the enemy. At a range of less than 100 yards, both ships opened fire. For the next few minutes, as guns roared, timbers split asunder and men screamed and died, the two ships hammering each other. Double-shotted round and grape from Hull's 24-pounder guns and 32-pounder carronades smashed into *Guerrière*. Soon the superior gunnery training and weight of fire of the Americans became apparent.

At about 7 pm, the two ships became locked in a deadly embrace. Both commanders called for boarders, but rough seas made it impossible for anyone to cross. Murderous musketry fire killed several men on both ships and an American sharpshooter shot Dacres in the back. What he lacked in common sense, Dacres made up for in courage. He refused to be taken below. Soon nearly every sailor on the British ship's fo'c'sle had been picked off by American musket fire.

Meanwhile, the wind pushed the ships free of one another and two of *Guerrière*'s masts crashed to the deck, leaving her wallowing uncontrollably in the heavy swell. While her crew gallantly tried to effect repairs, *Constitution* lay a short distance off. When she returned to *Guerrière* 30 minutes later, Dacres realized the hopelessness of further resistance and struck his colours. What no Briton thought possible had happened: an American warship had defeated a British one.

Guerriere's gunnery had been appalling. Despite the ferocity of the action, *Constitution* suffered only seven dead and another seven wounded, mostly to musket fire. Much of the ship remained largely unharmed by *Guerrière*'s guns, earning her the nickname "Old Ironsides." *Guerrière*'s condition was much worse. American gunnery had incapacitated one-third of her crew; 15 were dead and another 63 wounded, several of them mortally. At least 30 round shot had penetrated her hull. By next morning, she was leaking so badly that Hull abandoned and burned her. Shortly afterwards she blew up and sank, watched by a humiliated Dacres. Hull set course for Boston with more than 200 British prisoners.

Both the Americans and the British overreacted to *Constitution*'s feat. The American captain and his sailors became instant heroes, acclaimed across the land. All that mattered, from the American public's point of view, was that one of their frigates had beaten a British one. In the triumphal boasting, the disparity between the two warships was conveniently not mentioned or else forgotten. From the British public's point of view, faith in their "unbeatable" navy was severely shaken. Most of the citizens of Halifax, *Guerrière*'s station, simply refused to believe the first rumours of the debacle.

Philip Broke learned of Dacres' defeat as he sailed into Halifax on September 20. He expressed anger at *Constitution*,

In August 1812 the American super frigate *Constitution* sank the British frigate *Guerrière*.

but thought Dacres "did his best, but *fortune* ran against him." He was convinced he could beat the big American frigates: "Their force is superior in ship and metal and number of men, but not in *skill* or *courage* equal." Dacres and his crew were exchanged for American prisoners and returned to Halifax on September 29, where several were drafted into *Shannon*. The day before his court martial, Dacres dined with Broke, who took the opportunity to learn all he could about the American ship and how she fought.

At his court martial, Dacres blamed his defeat on the early loss of his mizzenmast. Neither the superior American gunnery nor the decidedly inferior British fire were mentioned. The officers who sat in judgment were only too willing to accept a reasonable explanation for the defeat, and "unanimously and honourably acquitted [Dacres] of all blame on account of her capture." No one made any effort to learn lessons from the fiasco. At least the Admiralty started to reinforce the North American Squadron, but this alone would not prove enough to beat the Americans at sea.

Two months later, on October 18, the British gun-brig *Frolic* (16 guns) encountered the sloop-of-war *Wasp* (18 guns) north of Bermuda. The two ships fought viciously, broadside to broadside, in a high swell for nearly 45 minutes before *Frolic* struck her colours. *Wasp* suffered five dead and five wounded, while more than half of *Frolic*'s sailors were casualties, some 15 killed and 47 wounded. Elation rebounded throughout America: her sailors had bested the Royal Navy again, this time in an even match, and Britain's naval prestige had endured another blow.

Then, a mere week later, on October 25, Captain Stephen Decatur of the super-frigate *United States* (44 guns) sailed from Boston and found the frigate *Macedonian* (38 guns) off Madeira. Decatur opened fire at 10 am and *Macedonian* struck her colours at 11:20 am. *Constitution*'s hull received only two or three balls compared to more than 100 in *Macedonian*'s shattered hull. The Americans had five fatalities and seven wounded; 38 British were killed and 66 wounded, more than a third of *Macedonian*'s complement.

As the first year of the war ended, Captain William Bainbridge relieved Hull as commander of *Constitution* and encountered the frigate *Java* (38 guns) off Brazil on December 29. In the hard-fought action that followed, British casualties amounted to 24 dead and 100 wounded. The Americans suffered nine dead and 25 wounded. Back in Boston, the citizens feted *Constitution*'s crew as the latest national heroes, while the British descended into even deeper despondency. Some Britons were beginning to recognize what the disparity in size and armament between the American and British frigates really meant, but their humiliation was not yet complete.

The fifth and final devastating single-ship action occurred on February 24, 1813, off British Guiana. Master Commandant (roughly equivalent to Commander) James Lawrence, of the sloop-of-war *Hornet* (18 guns), encountered Captain William Peake, commanding the aptly named brig-of-war *Peacock* (18 guns), known as "The Yacht" because of her brilliant appearance.

Peake believed more in gleaming paint and shiny brass than gunnery practice. He even removed the "unsightly" shot lockers from his gun deck to provide an uninterrupted view of his ship's smooth, scrubbed planking. The two ships opened fire at pistol range with broadsides that sent them both reeling. *Peacock* struck her colours 11 minutes later. Peake and seven others were dead and 30 wounded, while only one American was dead and two others wounded.

Lawrence was at sea for a total of 145 days and captured five ships. He replaced Bainbridge as the latest American hero. New Yorkers wined and dined "Captain Jim" and his crew when they arrived in the city in March. He received the freedom of the city and promotion to captain. On May 6, the navy ordered Lawrence to report to Boston to take command of the frigate *Chesapeake*, then completing refit, even though Secretary of the Navy William Jones had told him two days previously that he would be given *Constitution*. Lawrence was disappointed and dejected, deprived of what he assumed rightfully belonged to him. He complained bitterly but reluctantly complied. He could not have suspected that his new command would lead to defeat and disaster.

In the space of six months, the upstart United States Navy had defeated five Royal Navy warships decisively through superior skill and fighting ability. About the only quality the British ships did not lack was the courage of their crews. But despite American successes, in February 1813, Secretary Jones, fearing the Royal Navy still posed a threat to his few ships, ordered his commanders to cruise singly to avoid the possibility of a fleet action, since "our great inferiority in naval strength does not permit us to meet them."

On the British side, the Admiralty issued confidential instructions in July regarding future encounters, stating they did not conceive that "any of His Majesty's frigates should attempt to engage, single-handed, the larger class of American ships, which, though they may be called frigates, are of a size, complement and weight of metal much beyond that class and more resembling line-of-battle ships." At the very time the United States decided to avoid fleet actions, Britain was discouraging single-ship engagements. Naval strategy was deadlocked.

The deadlock would eventually be broken by the tall, well-built and red-haired Captain Philip Bowes Vere Broke. Broke assumed command of the newly built 150-foot-long *Shannon* (38 guns) on September 16, 1806, one week after his thirtieth birthday. Two previous *Shannons* had been wrecked at sea after short careers, causing some crewmen to mutter gloomily about an unlucky ship. Such would not be the case with Broke in charge. For the next five years, *Shannon* sailed European waters. Then in August 1811, new orders directed him and another frigate to join Vice Admiral Sawyer's squadron at Halifax in response to the *Little Belt* incident. Broke arrived at the headquarters of the North American Squadron on September 24, to find a tense atmosphere in the town and aboard the ships. Citizens and sailors alike expected war with the United States any day.

War did not break out for another 10 months, however, and *Shannon* spent most of that time cruising with *Guerrière* between Halifax and Bermuda, escorting convoys. Naturally gregarious, Broke also became involved in the social life of the station. In early 1812, Provo William Parry Wallis, a Halifax native, joined *Shannon* as Second Lieutenant. Although only 21 years of age, the tall, broad-shouldered and remarkably good-looking Wallis had already fought in two frigate actions against the French. He developed an immediate respect and admiration for his new captain, which later developed into a life-long affection.

Broke was a good leader and a good trainer. He was also a rarity among British naval officers: he believed in continuous gunnery training and constant practice. Ever since his time as a midshipman, he was fascinated by the application of scientific principles to naval gunnery, a subject the majority of the navy considered irrelevant. For most officers, the art of naval gunnery simply consisted of laying a ship so close alongside an enemy that the shot could not possibly miss. Broke's unbounded enthusiasm for gunnery coincided with a general decline in its standard throughout the Royal Navy. Perhaps Britain had been victorious at sea for far too long.

During his six years as *Shannon's* commander, the meticulous and thorough Broke put his gunnery theories into practice. He designed "dispart sights"—little notched wooden saddles—and fitted them on top of his gun barrels above the trunnions. They formed a second and forward sight for a gun captain to line up with the main sight, enabling him to obtain a more accurate line to the target than simply aiming along the top of the barrel. That was the method employed by *Guerrière* when most of her shots missed *Constitution*. Broke also fitted elevation scales to each gun to improve ranging, and had the deck behind every gun marked in degrees for concentrated fire. Other ships used some of these innovations; none but *Shannon* adopted them all.

No other captain practiced gunnery drills as frequently or as stringently as the intelligent, thoughtful Broke. He exercised his crew twice a day at sea, except for Saturday and Sunday. At a time when the Admiralty restricted ship's captains in the amount of shot they could use, Broke held live target practice twice a week, paying for the extra powder and shot himself, plus a pound of tobacco for any gunner who hit a floating canvas target. His gunners usually cut the canvas to ribbons. Broke, who described himself as a poor man, spent a lot of money on tobacco.

He wanted to ensure that every round fired struck the enemy's corresponding gun deck, no matter how badly his own ship was rolling or listing. He considered it a fault if any shot went above or below the sailors on an opponent's gun decks. Broke did not want to merely disable or sink ships; he wanted to kill as many of the enemy's men as possible. To do this, he needed the greatest power of horizontal fire in all situations.

Broke's adversary in the encounter to come was James Lawrence. Proud, tall, with an athletic build and a handsome, manly face, Lawrence assumed command of *Chesapeake* on May 20, 1813, four months short of his thirty-second birthday. The same length as *Shannon*, *Chesapeake* had a reputation as an unlucky ship, dating back to her launching in 1799 when she struck her slipway twice before hitting the water. *Chesapeake* had grounded several times and shipboard accidents had caused numerous injuries and fatalities. Then there was the notorious incident with *Leopard*, by far the worst stain on her career.

At the Boston Navy Yard in Charlestown, Lawrence found *Chesapeake* unready to sail due to a shortage of men and materials, which heightened his already demoralized state. Some of the crew assembled so far seemed a bad lot, the "sweepings" of the dockyard. However, the thought of going to sea again energized him, and he drove everyone to make *Chesapeake* ready. An impulsive man, he was chafing to get into action once again, hoping to advance his cause for command of *Constitution*, a burning desire he still harboured. In the 12 days before he sailed, Lawrence did his best to ensure *Chesapeake* and his sailors were up to the task ahead. By the end of May, Captain Jim had done all he could. He was ready to go out and meet the enemy.

Philip Broke felt the loss of *Guerrière* deeply and her defeat continued to prey on his mind. He wanted to show the impertinent Yankees what a good British ship could do. *Shannon* was rated at 38 guns, but Broke loaded 52 aboard, including some old brass 6-pounder long guns he had uncovered in the dockyard stores at Halifax. In early April, *Shannon*, in company with the frigate *Tenedos* (38 guns), arrived off Boston to reconnoitre the enemy port. After a few days spent spot observing and gathering intelligence, Broke discovered four United States Navy warships in harbour under the command of Commodore John Rodgers: *President* and *Congress* ready for sea, *Constitution* stripped down and the lately arrived *Chesapeake* undergoing repairs to her masts.

Broke sent repeated challenges to Rodgers to come out and meet him in single combat, promising to send away any other British ships. For whatever reason, Rodgers did not rise to the challenge, and Broke continued to cruise Massachusetts Bay. On May 24, he learned that *Chesapeake*, under her new captain, was almost ready for sea. Broke felt sure that Lawrence, with his reputation for hot-headedness, would accept the challenge, so he sent *Tenedos* off on an independent mission.

Aboard *Chesapeake*, rated for 36 guns but carrying 49, newly promoted Second Lieutenant Augustus Ludlow wrote to his brother, noting, "The ship is in better order for battle than I ever saw before." The next day, a chance meeting at sea with the Halifax privateer *Sir John Sherbrooke* allowed Broke to reinforce his crew with 22 young Irishmen. The men had been taken off the little British brig *Duck* by the American privateer *Governor Plumer*. *Sherbrooke* had subsequently captured the American raider and was on her way home with her prize when she came across *Shannon*.

On May 31, Broke composed a letter of his own, choosing his words carefully to convey exactly the right meaning to Lawrence, requesting him to "do me the favour to meet the *Shannon* . . . ship to ship, to try the fortune of our respective flags." He noted that his ship "mounts 24 guns upon her broadside, and one light boat gun; 18-pounders upon her maindeck, and 32-pound carronades on her quarterdeck and forecastle; and is manned with a complement of 300 seamen and boys, (a large proportion of the latter)." He assured Lawrence, "I will send all other ships beyond the power of interfering with us, and meet you wherever it is agreeable to you."

Broke went on to point out, "My proposals are highly advantageous to you, as you cannot proceed to sea singly in the *Chesapeake*, without imminent risk of being crushed by the superior force of the numerous British squadrons which are now abroad," and asked Lawrence not to "imagine that I am urged by personal vanity to the wish of meeting the *Chesapeake*; or that I depend only upon your personal ambition for your acceding to this invitation: we have both nobler motives." Finally, he requested Lawrence to "favour me with a speedy reply. We are short of provisions and water, and cannot stay here long." Broke stopped a fishing schooner the next day, June 1, to carry his challenge to Lawrence. As the boat made its way to shore, *Chesapeake* was already under way: Lawrence never received Broke's written challenge.

When Lawrence ascertained that the strange sail off the harbour that bright, sunny morning was British, he addressed all hands: "Chesapeakes, an English frigate is in sight and it is my intention to go out and bring her into action. We must die first before we see [our] flag dishonoured. Remember the old *Hornet* and that glorious victory, and when we close this Englishman, *Peacock* her, my brave lads, *Peacock* her!"

Around 12:30 pm, *Chesapeake* made her way toward the bay, flying a white banner proclaiming "FREE TRADE AND SAILOR'S RIGHTS." Spectators lined the waterfront and rooftops, while a flotilla of small boats accompanied her, anxious to witness the spectacle of yet another British defeat. A wharf had even been cleared to tie up *Shannon* after the battle, and preparations started for a glorious victory supper.

Broke watched *Chesapeake* with undisguised delight. He had done everything possible to prepare for battle. All he could do now was head further out to sea, away from any potential shore boarding parties should *Shannon* become crippled. Wearing a shiny black top hat for better protection than afforded by his uniform cocked hat, Broke spoke to his men, reminding them the recent American victories were due mainly to a disparity of force: "But they have gone further. They have said and published in their newspapers that the English have forgotten how to fight. You will let them know today that there are Englishmen in the *Shannon* who still know how to fight."

His final instructions to his men concerned their conduct during the coming battle: "Don't try to dismast her. Fire into her quarters; maindeck into maindeck; quarterdeck into quarterdeck. Kill the men and the ship is yours. . . . Don't cheer. Go quietly to your quarters. I feel sure you will all do your duty; and remember, you have the blood of hundreds of your countrymen to avenge." Throughout the ship, the crew solemnly turned to their final preparations for the coming battle.

At 5:40 pm, with both ships moving at a speed of three to four knots, *Chesapeake*, some 50 yards off *Shannon*'s starboard quarter and looking as if she might pass across Broke's stern, altered course to run alongside *Shannon*'s starboard side within pistol range. At that moment, Broke knew he had the American ship. He called out orders for his maindeck gunners to fire when they had *Chesapeake*'s second maindeck gun port in their sights.

At 5:50 pm, *Shannon*'s aftermost maindeck 18-pounder, No. 14, fired. The round shot crashed through the solid timbers above *Chesapeake*'s second gun, into the soft flesh of the gun crew, splattering blood and scattering body parts. Jagged, razor-sharp splinters, the missiles feared most by sailors, flew across the deck at musket-shot velocity, digging deeply into heads, torsos and limbs. The deck instantly became slippery with blood and gore. Survivors tugged at mangled bodies, pulling them clear so that they could fire the gun. They sent the wounded below and the dead into the sea.

Within a minute, the remainder of *Shannon*'s starboard battery methodically opened fire as *Chesapeake* came into view, displaying the same deadly accuracy as No. 14 gun. Each maindeck British gun, loaded with two solid shots or shot and grape, and her quarterdeck carronades, loaded with one shot and one grape, spread destruction aft as *Chesapeake* passed by, sailing a knot faster. The 9-pounders assigned to dismantle *Chesapeake*'s wheel quickly dispatched the quartermaster and all who leapt forward to replace him. A well-aimed shot from a British topman hit Lawrence in the right leg below the knee. Blood poured down the pale white breeches of the spotless uniform he was wearing for the occasion.

At 5:52 pm, Lawrence luffed his ship (brought her head to wind) to take some way off, causing *Chesapeake* to turn away and veer her stern-half toward *Shannon*. All the American guns were in bearing by now, and the guns of the surviving midships and after crews pounded *Shannon*. Most shots hit below the maindeck, striking the copper sheathing exposed above the waterline. A few found their target, however, smashing into gun crews and sending limbs and pieces of flesh flying. Screams and shrieks of agony joined the cheering and cursing of blackened, bloody, sweating sailors, as the great guns thundered and small arms crackled. The smell of powder filled the air, already thick with choking, gritty smoke.

As *Chesapeake* overtook *Shannon,* the two ships sailed yardarm to yardarm, sweeping each other's decks with ball and bar shot, grape and canister, star and chain shot, musket and pistol bullet. The metal tore through timber, canvas, rope and flesh alike. As Broke lifted his foot to step over something on the deck, a 32-pounder ball from *Chesapeake* ricocheted off a 9-pounder swivel gun and flew on, passing between his legs. The gun captain fell to the deck with both kneecaps fractured, while the loader took grapeshot in his lower abdomen. He loaded the gun, and then fell to the deck, begging those nearby to put a hand into his dreadful wound and remove the shot. He died shortly afterward.

At 5:54 pm, the American ship lost way and began to drift back towards *Shannon.* A midshipman in *Shannon*'s maintop hurled a grenade down onto *Chesapeake*'s quarterdeck, where it blew up a box of ammunition. The explosion added to the nightmare scene, killing or wounding several nearby seamen and starting a fire. Broke ran forward, saw *Chesapeake* gathering sternway, and realized she would soon collide with him. If he could hold off, he could rake her repeatedly from a distance and finish her. The hand grenade fire subsided a little, but Broke was worried that flames in *Chesapeake*'s rigging would spread to his ship. *Shannon* moved away, but slowly.

Meanwhile, *Shannon*'s guns continued to hammer *Chesapeake,* while Royal Marines' deadly musket fire swept her deck. The American sailors scrambled forward, away from the fire raging at her stern, although their Marines held firm. Broke realized that *Shannon* was not going to get clear and called for boarders; at the same time, Lawrence saw that the ships would collide and called for his. However, on *Chesapeake* there were no unwounded officers left on the upper deck to rally his decimated ranks. Then *Chesapeake*'s port quarter ground into *Shannon,* about 50 feet from the bow, and the ships' rigging became entangled.

Through a gap in the smoke and haze, Marine Second Lieutenant John Law caught sight of a tall man in dress uniform on *Chesapeake*'s quarterdeck. Assuming it to be the Yankee captain, he grabbed a musket and fired. It took him three shots before he hit

The British frigate *Shannon* defeated the American frigate *Chesapeake* off Boston harbour in June 1813. The battle lasted only 15 minutes.

Lawrence. The American captain staggered and fell, clutching his groin. Blood spurted out between his fingers. In terrible pain, he continued to call for boarders. Acting Lieutenant William Cox reached Lawrence just as he fell. Cox was now the only uninjured officer on the upper deck, but did not know it. Instead of confirming the situation, Cox's only thought was for his captain, and he helped him below. As Cox carried him down, Lawrence gasped the famous words that would become the motto of the United States Navy: "Don't give up the ship!"

Broke, still forward, looked across onto *Chesapeake*'s nearly empty quarterdeck, just over a yard away. He needed to act quickly. The American frigate was still being blown around by the wind. The two ships were barely touching and would not hold together for much longer. He had to get as many Shannons on her as possible before that happened. He was the nearest to the other ship. With a cry of "Follow me who can!" Broke drew his sword and took the unusual step for a Royal Navy captain of jumping across to *Chesapeake.*

Other Shannons quickly followed, including a group of Halifax volunteers, who had already made themselves useful by helping the marines with return fire against American marksmen aloft. *Chesapeake*'s acting chaplain, Samuel Livermore, stood his ground. He aimed a pistol at Broke, fired and missed, then attempted to strike him with the empty weapon. Broke swung his sword upwards in a backhand cut, nearly severing the man's arm. When he later learned he had wounded a man of God, he was mortified.

A heavily armed group of Chesapeakes rallied on the fo'c'sle in an attempt to stop the British rush. Despite their greater numbers, the Shannons, armed mostly with cutlasses, could make no headway. Then a big, powerful Halifax man stepped forward and swung a handspike with such force that two Americans went spinning. The British drove the others back. At about that time the fragile hold between the two ships gave way and they drifted apart. In the minute or so they were locked together, about 70 Shannons gained *Chesapeake*. American resistance began to falter.

Suddenly, three Americans rushed Broke from behind. A British sailor yelled, and Broke turned in time to parry a pike thrust from the first man. He ran him through with his sword, but the second Chesapeake swung a musket that knocked off Broke's hat and thudded down on his shoulder. The third sailor slashed at Broke with a sabre, opening a four-inch gash in his scalp that parted the bone down to the brain cavity. Stunned, the British captain fell to the deck. Blood gushed from the wound and ran down the side of his face and neck. As one of the Americans tried to finish him off, some of Broke's crewmen quickly dispatched all three attackers.

Resistance on *Chesapeake* continued to weaken. When First Lieutenant George Watt ordered the Stars and Stripes hauled down and started to run up his white ensign, a shot of grape, mistakenly fired from *Shannon*, killed him and either killed or wounded five or six others. The British quickly recovered and succeeded in hoisting their ensign. On *Shannon*, Provo Wallis, in charge of the maindeck, immediately ordered his men to cease fire. By now, most surviving Americans were being driven below, with a few keeping up a

Captain Philip Broke of *Shannon* led the boarding party aboard *Chesapeake*. He wore a top hat for better protection than his naval cocked hat.

ragged musket fire. When Lawrence realized the *Chesapeake* was lost he cried, "Then blow her up! Blow the ship up!" But no one rushed to carry out his order. Broke, who was dizzy and barely conscious from his wound, ordered Third Lieutenant Charles Falkiner to call down to the Americans to surrender. The battle was over. It was 6:05 pm. Only 11 minutes had elapsed from the time No. 14 gun fired until Shannons boarded the American vessel. It took only another four minutes for the boarders to do their job, and for the Chesapeakes to surrender.

It was the bloodiest single-frigate action in history. Never before had so many men been slaughtered in so little time. The casualty rate was ten times that of the *United States/Macedonian* and *Constitution/Java* encounters.

Some 158 American shots struck *Shannon*, mostly in her side, with some damaging her rigging. Three officers and 20 men died in action, and another two officers and nine men died of wounds. Forty-three were wounded. More than half of those who boarded *Chesapeake* became casualties: six were killed and 34 were wounded, four fatally.

Some 362 British shots struck *Chesapeake*, mostly on her gun deck, disabling three guns, dismounting or damaging others and injuring her masts. Six officers and 42 men died fighting, while another three officers and 11 men died of wounds. Eighty-five suffered wounds and 320 became prisoners. And, in the end, no one had followed either of Lawrence's admonitions: first, to not give up the ship, and second, to blow her up.

The American spectators who witnessed the action could not believe their eyes when *Chesapeake*'s colours came down. When they returned to Boston, there was universal disbelief; the grand victory supper was cancelled. Almost immediately excuses were made to try to explain this unprecedented, inconceivable, utter defeat. Many of them survive as accepted fact, but they do not stand up under close examination. Augustus Ludlow, now acting first lieutenant, and recovering from his head wound, disdained his fellow officers who protested the battle had been won by some underhanded means; "We were fairly beaten," he remarked.

Willing hands carried a still-conscious Broke back to his cabin, where the ship's doctor gave him little hope for survival. Sailors also carried Lawrence over to the *Shannon* and placed him in the wardroom. Responsibility for getting the ship home fell to Wallis, the senior surviving uninjured officer. He put Lieutenant Falkiner in charge of *Chesapeake*, where, in Wallis's words, there were "upon the deck some hundreds of handcuffs in readiness for us, so we ornamented them with their own manacles." Falkiner transferred a number of Americans to *Shannon* for better control over the prisoners. While the surgeons and their assistants saw to the wounded, others committed the bodies of the fallen to the deep. Sailors tried to sluice blood, gore and scattered body parts off the decks of both ships.

Wallis wanted to get away from the coast as quickly as possible in case other American warships should come out of the harbour. He directed hurried efforts to make essential—though only temporary—repairs to both vessels to get them safely to Halifax. They sailed that evening. Fortunately, the weather remained fine, enabling the crew to make additional repairs during the voyage.

Lawrence's condition worsened when peritonitis set in due to the musket ball buried deep in his lower abdomen. He sunk into a delirious coma and died on June 4, just off Sambro Light at the entrance to Halifax Harbour.

Dense fog hindered the two ships for the next two days, and they did not enter the harbour until Whitsunday morning, June 6. News of their arrival spread quickly throughout the town. In St. Paul's Church, where the sermon had just begun, word passed quietly from pew to pew. The church soon emptied.

Seventeen-year-old Thomas Chandler Haliburton, who would later achieve fame as a judge and humourist, was one of those in the congregation. He described what happened as *Shannon* and *Chesapeake* made their way to the dockyard: "Every housetop and every wharf was crowded with groups of excited people, and as the ships successively passed, they were greeted with vociferous cheers. Halifax was never in such a state of excitement before or since." When the crowd realized Wallis was in command of *Shannon*, "this circumstance naturally added to the enthusiasm of the citizens, for they felt that, through him, they had some share in the honour of the achievement." A Royal Navy victory, and a resounding one, at last! British honour had been restored.

Wallis would not let the enthusiastic crowds who rowed out to *Shannon* board for fear of disturbing the injured Broke, so they pulled across to *Chesapeake* instead. Haliburton was among them:

> *Internally the scene was never to be forgotten by a landsman. The deck had not been cleaned, and the coils and folds of rope were steeped in gore as if in a slaughterhouse. She was a fir-built ship and her splinters had wounded nearly as many men as the Shannon's shot. Pieces of skin with pendant hair were adhering to the sides of the ship, and in one place I saw portions of fingers protruding. Altogether it was a scene of devastation as difficult to forget as to describe. It is one of the most painful reminiscences of my youth.*

Sailors took all the wounded to the Royal Naval Hospital, except for Broke, whom they carried to the Commissioner's House in the dockyard. Guards escorted the unwounded Chesapeakes to the prison on Melville Island. At 1:30 pm on June 8, sailors rowed the body of Captain James Lawrence across to the King's Wharf, to the firing of minute guns. In a solemn and elaborate ceremony, the band and funeral party of 300 soldiers from the 64th Regiment escorted the body to St. Paul's Cemetery, accompanied by the officers of the garrison, each of whom wore a black armband, together with the officers of the Royal Navy. Six naval captains acted as pallbearers. When the service ended, the firing party discharged three volleys over the grave.

Five days later, Augustus Ludlow, Lawrence's acting first lieutenant, took a turn for the worse and died of his wounds. He was buried near his captain. Of the Shannons who died after arriving in Halifax, two were buried in St. Paul's Cemetery and five in the dockyard's Naval Cemetery, where their communal grave is still marked by a pyramid-topped stone. Twelve hospitalized Chesapeakes who later died are thought to have been laid to rest in the Naval Cemetery alongside their former foes from *Shannon*. A memorial in their honour was erected in 1966.

On August 10, the American brig *Henry* of Salem arrived in Halifax under a flag of truce to retrieve the bodies of Lawrence and Ludlow. On August 19, their remains were removed at night and taken to Salem where they were reburied, along with seven crewmen from *Chesapeake*. But it was not to be their final resting place. On September 16, they were reburied once more, this time in Trinity Churchyard at the lower end of Broadway, after a solemn procession watched by 30,000 New Yorkers.

Despite the seriousness of his wound, Broke survived and returned to Britain with *Shannon*. Word of his victory preceded him, making the country wild with joy. He arrived at Portsmouth to a hero's welcome. The name *Shannon* eventually passed to a new ship, whose naval brigade served with distinction during the Indian Mutiny, 1857–58. One of her crew, Able Seaman William Hall from Hantsport, won the Victoria Cross at the Relief of Lucknow, becoming the first black, the first Nova Scotian and the third Canadian ever to achieve this rare distinction. His parents were among several hundred escaped slaves whom the British had conveyed from Chesapeake Bay plantations during the war.

On his return to England, Broke became in succession a Baronet, Knight Commander of the Order of the Bath and Rear Admiral. He received £2,449 in prize money from *Chesapeake*— not enough to make him rich, but sufficient to be comfortable. Although offered another command, Broke never served at sea again and retired to Broke Hall in Suffolk. The Admiralty consulted him frequently on gunnery matters, and eventually established naval gunnery schools. For the most part, however, he lived the quiet life of a country squire.

He died peacefully in his sleep on January 2, 1841, at 65 years of age, after undergoing surgery to relieve the congestion on his brain caused by his old head wound. In the Broke Chapel in his village church, a memorial tablet bearing an inscription from the Lords of the Admiralty notes his "professional skill and gallantry in battle, which has seldom been equalled and certainly never surpassed."

The Admiralty promoted Lieutenants Provo Wallis and Charles Falkiner to Commanders for their part in the action. Wallis went on to even higher rank. The sovereign made him a Knight Commander of the Order of the Bath and subsequently raised him within the order. He became Admiral of the Fleet in 1877 and was known as "The Father of the British Fleet." By the time he died in 1892, at the age of 101, he had served an incredible 88 years in the Royal Navy and was one of the last survivors of the days of iron men and wooden ships. Many other Nova Scotians joined the Royal Navy, and six of them, besides Wallis, rose to the rank of admiral.

The United States Navy soon had an opportunity to repay the courtesies the Royal Navy had showed Lawrence's remains. Commander Samuel Blyth had attended the American captain's funeral and immediately afterwards sailed from Halifax in command of the brig *Boxer* (14 guns) to harry the coast of Maine.

At dawn on September 6, after nearly three months of cruising, during which he captured a couple of small prizes, Blyth was sighted off Portland by Lieutenant William Burrows, who was commanding the brig *Enterprise* (16 guns). In a sharp, 30-minute action, *Enterprise* turned *Boxer* into a wreck, killing or wounding one-third of her crew, including Blyth, who was felled by an 18-pound shot through the body during the first broadsides. In the same action, British grapeshot killed Burrows.

The senior surviving officer on *Enterprise* took his ship and her prize into Portland. The bodies of the two captains were rowed ashore to the sound of minute guns and borne through the streets in a procession escorted by Portland's militia and regular troops, as well as every available civil, military and naval official in the city and large numbers of ordinary citizens. They were buried next to each other in Portland's cemetery, where Blyth's men placed a stone over his grave. It was another example of the rigid code of manners the forces of the two sides observed toward each other throughout the war.

2

PRIZE, PROFIT AND PRIVATEERS

Just what was Enos Collins up to? Why had he spent £440 at prize auction in November 1811 on the small, foul-smelling and cramped former tender to a Spanish slaver that went by the name of *Black Joke*? She was too narrow for bulk cargo and definitely unsuitable for the fishery. The shrewd Collins was not normally known to waste his money; he was too able and too smart for that. His colleagues decided the ship's name was right—this must be some kind of joke. Only it wasn't. Collins had plans for his latest acquisition, plans that would bear fruit in the war that he saw brewing between Britain and the United States.

Enos Collins had a knack for picking the right opportunities. Born in 1774 in Liverpool, Nova Scotia, he served at sea for the early part of his career, gaining not only experience, but also amassing the start of what would eventually become a vast fortune. At the turn of the century, Collins became acting first lieutenant in the Liverpool privateer *Charles Mary Wentworth*, sailing the Caribbean trade routes in search of lucrative French merchantmen. He returned to his hometown with enough money to set himself up as a shipowner and trader.

Britain's war with Revolutionary France not only started his fortune, but also helped it grow. During the two-and-a-half-year French siege of Cadiz, Spain, the British and Spanish armies— allies since 1808—were running out of provisions. The battle was

Enos Collins was at various times a privateer, a
shipowner, a merchant and a banker.

close to being lost. In 1810, Collins sent three shiploads of food
across the ocean. The British purchased them and Collins made a
huge profit. He moved to Halifax in November 1811 and became a
merchant, in partnership with Joseph Allison.

Black Joke was captured by British warships enforcing the ban on
slave trading—illegal in the British Empire since 1807. The Royal
Navy sent her to Halifax, where the Court of Vice-Admiralty condemned her and put her up for sale to the highest bidder in the
rooms of the Spread Eagle tavern at the foot of Salter Street.

Built in the United States, *Black Joke* was a compact little 53-
foot-long black-hulled schooner, registered at only 67 tons. Her
two masts, slanted back at a rakish angle, carried both fore-and-aft
sails, while her foremast carried square sails as well. Three large

headsails swept back from her exaggerated bowsprit. She seemed built more for racing than for commerce.

Give that *Black Joke*'s decks still carried the stench of her latest prohibited cargo, Collins had to fumigate her with a concoction of vinegar, tar and brimstone before he could use her. He rechristened her *Liverpool Packet* and put the speedy little schooner on a run carrying a few passengers and mail between Halifax and his hometown, where her co-owners Benjamin Knaut and John and James Barss lived. It was certainly no way to get rich, but circumstances would soon change with the outbreak of the war. *Liverpool Packet* would become the most lucrative letter-of-marque ship ever to sail out of a Canadian port—and the nemesis of American merchant shipping.

During the War of 1812, privateers—both ships and men—were Nova Scotia's main contribution to the war effort. Several hundred Bluenosers sailed in as many as three dozen of these little ships and brought more than 200 prizes into port. Overall, privateers did little to win the war, but they did serve as an auxiliary naval force and gathered valuable intelligence for the Royal Navy about American strength and ship movements.

Privateers also made several people, like Enos Collins, wealthy. Collins probably cleared £30,000 from his investments in privateers alone. However, privateering was not always a successful venture. A third of the province's privateers took no prizes at all, and only about half of them seized more than two enemy ships. Seven of the most successful privateers accounted for nearly three-quarters of all captures. It was also a risky business: almost a quarter of the ships that sailed from Nova Scotia's ports were captured, burned or lost.

Despite the risks, several men were willing to sail as privateers, or to put up the money to buy, outfit and bond the ships. The lure of seizing a lucrative prize was too great to resist. In order to spread the costs—and the risks—ownership of privateers was usually shared between two or more partners.

Privateering and profiteering went hand in hand. Privateers seized American merchant ships and their cargoes. Merchants and traders bought them at auctions in Halifax and promptly resold them. In many cases, they even resold to the Americans their own goods. Sometimes the same durable goods were captured and sold more than once.

The War of 1812 essentially saw both the zenith and the conclusion of privateering. It allowed Nova Scotian shipowners to use their vessels and crews during a period when wartime conditions restricted regular shipping. The practice became very much a part of the life of several coastal communities, offering opportunities for speculation, service and excitement.

Privateering had been a family business for many years, and many of the men who sailed as privateers were related by blood or marriage, none more so than those from Liverpool. They received financial backing from relatives ashore, and in no other town in the province, or in all the Maritimes, was there as much speculation in privateering undertakings. Collins was the major investor.

Privateering—also known as commerce raiding and *guerre de course*—was and is often considered as little more than government-licenced piracy. It had a tradition stretching back some six centuries. In its simplest form, it was a type of commercial warfare against an enemy's trade rather than his territory; and depended on warships and privately owned ships attacking his cargo-carrying vessels. A privateer was usually a converted merchantman ship, although occasionally one was built specifically for the purpose.

Besides the normal stores for any cruise, a privateer was also fitted out with the necessary implements of war to turn her into a fighting vessel. Larger ships were equipped with carriage cannons of various sizes. Smaller swivel guns were also used. Usually these were carronades—short, snub-nosed cannons that could be devastating at close range. Although less accurate than long guns, privateers generally preferred carronades. They were lighter, used less powder, took up less room and were cheaper to buy. They were particularly good for the close-in work preferred by privateers. They carried powder, shot, cutlasses, muskets, pistols and boarding pikes as well.

Despite her fighting equipment, a privateering vessel was never intended to be used to fight anything her own size and, with any luck, she could run away if necessary.

Before a ship could legitimately embark on a privateering cruise, her owners and captain required a licence, called a letter of marque, issued by the province's lieutenant-governor. Unfortunately for them, Lieutenant-Governor Sherbrooke initially did not think he had the authority to issue letters of marque on his own, and referred the matter to Britain. When the British finally issued the necessary documents, they specified the enemy to be the French and other "enemies of the Crown," which referred to the Americans without actually naming them.

In some cases, the licence might set restrictions as to time and territory—stating when and where privateering was valid. Once it became obvious that the Americans were serious about the war, Sherbrooke issued his own letters of marque. They permitted privateers "by force of arms to attack, surprise, seize and take all ships and vessels, goods, wares and merchandise, chattels and effects belonging to any persons inhabiting within any of the territories of the United States of America," except for any harbours "within shot of the cannon of princes or states in amity with His Majesty."

Operating without such a document was considered an act of piracy, the penalty for which was hanging. Additionally, owners had to post a bond of £1,500 to £3,000 for good behaviour. Vessels or cargo captured by a letter-of-marque ship did not become the property of the captor until the Court of Vice-Admiralty at Halifax adjudicated on the matter, sometimes several months after the capture. All captured ships and their cargoes were sent before the court. If found to have been taken legally, they were sold at public auction. But sometimes the judgment could go against the privateer and the prize be declared unlawful.

Ships' owners, who invested the risk capital for a cruise, normally took half of the net profits, while judges and court officials received hefty commissions. Officers and sailors did not receive wages, but were given shares in any prizes they captured, based on the number left after the owners and the captain had taken theirs.

Nova Scotia sent several successful, authorized letter-of-marque privateers to sea. Others do not appear to have been issued commissions or may have been alternate names used by those that were authorized. Records of some of Nova Scotia's privateers are missing, but details exist on the majority of them, ranging from the tiny schooner *Crown* to the imposing brig *Sir John Sherbrooke*, named for Nova Scotia's lieutenant-governor.

Halifax's *Crown* was not only the smallest provincial privateer, but also the smallest in all of Canada. She may even have been the most diminutive of all the British vessels that put to sea against the Americans. Commissioned in February 1813 and captained by Solomon Jennings, *Crown* was 40 feet long and carried a crew of 30, many of them boys.

It was said that even a boy could not stand up below deck without bumping his head, and fully grown members of the crew had to come up on deck to have the room to put on their seaboots. Most of her crew had to sleep on the deck under canvas. For armament, she carried a single 9-pound carronade.

After two days at sea during her first cruise in April 1813, *Crown* sighted a ship 10 miles southwest of Cape Sable that was five times her size. *Crown* pursued her, eventually capturing her after a two-and-a-half-hour chase. It was the brigantine *Sibae* of Boston, badly off track on a homeward-bound voyage from Savannah, Georgia, with a cargo of cotton bales. Jennings put a prize crew aboard her, at the same time transferring *Sibae*'s seven crew members to his ship in handcuffs. Unluckily for the *Crown*'s crew and owners, the Royal Navy sloop-of-war *Atalante* (18 guns) arrived on the scene shortly afterwards, brusquely claiming joint capture by virtue of having also been in pursuit of the American ship.

The privateer's protests so irritated Captain Frederick Hickey that he forced two of them into the Royal Navy on the spot—an unusual action against privateersmen—by uttering the words, "I press you here and now in the King's name and for the King's service." Pressing privateers was probably one of the more ill-advised acts committed by the British navy, as these men perhaps contributed to the war and Britain's cause just as effectively as serving the guns of a man-of-war. It was neither the first, nor the last, foolish decision the Admiralty would make.

The Court of Vice-Admiralty in Halifax did not hear the case of the disputed *Sibae* for several months. In the meantime, Jennings put a request into Shelburne to discharge his prisoners and replace his impressed crewmen, but three of his sailors deserted out of fear of impressment. Jennings put to sea immediately to prevent further desertions. With only 19 men and boys aboard he headed for the coast of Maine, where he captured two or three small coasters.

Then the tables turned for the little *Crown*. On April 30, Jennings chased the sloop *Increase*, fitted out with six guns and a crew of 80 as a decoy to lure the Royal Navy's man-of-war schooner *Bream*, which had burned several coasters. Instead, she lured *Crown* into a trap and forced Jennings to surrender after a one-sided battle that saw her colours shot away twice.

In a letter, written from a Maine jail to his ship's owners, Jennings expressed his amazement about the fight: "What is most wonderful to relate is that there is [sic] about 300 balls in our hull and spars, the sails and rigging of both vessels wonderfully cut to pieces, a number of balls through our hats and cloathes, yet there is not a man either killed or wounded on either side."

The Court of Vice-Admiralty eventually ruled the taking of *Sibae* a joint capture, and the navy and the privateer shared £5,063 in prize money. *Atalante*'s interference had indirectly ended *Crown*'s career as a privateer, but fortunately for Jennings and his men, the Americans seemed to have more respect for privateers than Hickey did. They treated them well and at the first opportunity returned them to Halifax during a prisoner exchange.

Two other privateers commissioned in Halifax in 1813, the schooners *Weazel* and *George,* were less lucky than *Crown*. The 45-ton *Weazel* was a "pinky," a type of small, exceptionally seaworthy schooner. She was heavily armed with a 9-pounder, four 4-pounders and a pair of swivels. Usually she sailed with a crew of 35, although at times may have set forth with as few as eight.

Under George William Anderson, she apprehended several prizes that summer: the sloops *Franklin* and *Leonidas*, and the schooners *Calson*, *Don Carlos* and *Minerva*. In *Minerva*, prize-master William Smith found over $3,800 hidden in bags in her sand ballast. Unfortunately for the privateers, she sailed with a British licence from Barbados and the prize court gave the ship back to her American owners, including all the money on board.

George had even less luck. A 112-ton vessel, with a crew of 60, that mounted six 9-pounders and a pair of swivels, she departed Halifax on August 27, 1813, on a two-month cruise under John Gilchrist. For her four owners, she made only one capture: the Spanish two-decker *San Domingo* en route from Havana to Portsmouth, New Hampshire. As prize-master James Boatland brought her in, he survived severe gales, only to lose her on the Jeddore Ledges on October 9. Such were the risks of privateering.

On June 27, 1812, nine days after the American declaration of war, word reached Halifax that Britain was at war with the United States. Enos Collins and his partners immediately decided to take *Liverpool Packet* out of passenger service and convert her into a privateer. The crew installed five rusty cannons that had been serving as gate posts on the waterfront, one a 12-pounder and the others 6-pounders. They were big guns for a ship her size—4-pounders would have been normal—but they gave her an extra punch that served her well over the next three years. Collins also strengthened the decks against enemy cannon fire, and installed steel-clad powder magazines and shot lockers.

The ship left Liverpool under her first captain, John Freeman, on August 30, 1812, bound for Georges Bank off the coast of Massachusetts. Meanwhile another Maritime privateer, *General Smyth* of Saint John, had already taken the first prize of the war when she captured an American ship on August 13. *Liverpool Packet* had some catching up to do. Freeman took his first prize on September 7: the 325-ton merchant ship *Middlesex*, bound for New York from Liverpool, England, with a mixed cargo. He sent her to Halifax for adjudication by the Court of Vice-Admiralty. The next day he captured *Factor*, a ship more than four times the size of the *Liverpool Packet*. Her load of Port wine, destined for Providence, Rhode Island, had already been pillaged by a British privateer, but enough remained for the crew to get drunk.

Joseph Barss Jr. of Liverpool was already an experienced privateer when the War of 1812 broke out.

When *Liverpool Packet* returned to her homeport, Freeman was not in command. For some reason—perhaps the drunken episode with the crew—Joseph Barss Jr., brother of two of Collins's partners, was in charge. Although a much younger man than Freeman, Barss, at 36, was an experienced privateer from a privateering family, having sailed on *Charles Mary Wentworth* and commanded *Rover* a few years earlier. As captain of *Liverpool Packet*, he set an amazing record for taking prizes.

Barss headed for Massachusetts Bay, off Cape Cod, where he thought the pickings would be richer than those on Georges Bank. He was right. In one week in October, he took 11 vessels. He followed this up by taking nine fishing schooners, carrying cargo worth $50,000, in one day. The New England press reacted with indignation, and demanded that the navy take action against this lone predator.

Barss soon suffered from an embarrassment of riches and had to limit himself to manning and sending only his most important prizes to Halifax for adjudication, releasing the others. After a refit, *Liverpool Packet* was back off Cape Cod on December 10. Within three weeks, Barss captured eight or nine vessels with a value totalling between $70,000 and $90,000. The newspapers continued to press for his capture while Barss and his crew spent Christmas at home, savouring their new-found wealth. Three and a half months work had netted them and the owners more than $100,000 in prize money—equivalent to more than $3,000,000 today. When they returned to sea in February, normally a sparse time for shipping in northern waters, they took an additional 33 prizes over a two-month period. But Barss's luck was about to run out.

On June 11, 1813, a larger ship, the American privateer *Thomas* spotted *Liverpool Packet* off the coast of Maine and gave chase. *Liverpool Packet* had only 36 hands left aboard after other crewmen had been sent to Halifax with captured prizes. *Thomas* carried a larger crew and was more heavily armed, with ten carriage guns and four swivels. Barss turned and fled as Captain Shaw pursued him.

Liverpool Packet, the most successful privateer in Canadian history and of either side during the War of 1812. She captured over 100 prizes in 22 months.

As Barss ran, he moved his 12-pounder to the stern and fired off every 12-pound shot he had, in an attempt to stop Shaw. He even threw his other guns overboard to lighten the ship, but the bigger privateer continued to gain on him. After six hours, Captain Barss—faced with the inevitable—struck his colours. Despite the surrender, Shaw's men stormed *Liverpool Packet*, firing their muskets. In the exchange that followed, sailors on both sides were killed before the two captains were able to stop further bloodshed.

Shaw took the smaller Nova Scotian schooner to her homeport of Portsmouth, New Hampshire, where he received an ecstatic welcome. Unfortunately, the public's delight was accompanied by a thirst for revenge. During the War of 1812 both sides normally treated their prisoners with respect, allowing paroles and exchanges. The parole system was a practical solution to the problems of holding large groups of prisoners of war. Developed over a long period, parole had all the advantages of removing the enemy's soldiers and sailors from further action, without the effort and expense of looking after them. In return for not being imprisoned, the captive gave his *parole d'honneur*, or word of honour, that he would not take up arms against his captors.

The crew of *Liverpool Packet*, however, had humiliated too many New England seamen. Barss and his men were paraded through the streets of Portsmouth, shackled in irons, as jeering crowds threatened them. The authorities threw them into jail, where Barss was singled out for especially severe treatment. He was kept in fetters and fed only hardtack and water. When he was finally parolled, after months in jail, the Americans first extracted an affidavit from him promising not to engage in privateering against American ships ever again. He kept his word, and later sailed as master of a schooner that traded with the West Indies.

Ironically, this ship, *Wolverine*, was previously *Thomas*, the very vessel that had ended his privateering career. After *Thomas's* capture by a British man-of-war, condemnation by the Court of Vice-Admiralty and sale at auction in August 1813, she had been fitted out as a privateer by some Liverpool backers. She sailed on September 5 under Captain Charles Shea, heavily armed with five

9-pounders, two 6-pounders, four 4-pounders, a 24-pounder and four swivels for good measure. Shea and his successor, John Roberts Jr., took 15 prizes between them by December. *Wolverine* then ceased her privateering career and became an armed merchant ship under Barss's command.

Shortly after he returned from his one West Indies trip, Barss gave up the sea for good and retired to a farm in the Annapolis Valley. *Wolverine* once again briefly became a privateer, but was lost at sea after the war with all hands.

Meanwhile, the Americans put *Liverpool Packet* up for auction. She was quickly bought and fitted out again for privateering. Her new owners rechristened her *Young Teazer's Ghost*, in memory of *Young Teazer*, which had in turn been named after her predecessor, *Teazer*.

Teazer had been a small, two-gun New York privateer, crewed by 50 sailors. The Royal Navy captured her early in the war after she had been privateering for five months. They considered her to be such "small fish" that they burned her. Among her parolled officers was her captain, Frederick Johnson, by all accounts a particularly unsavoury character. He was rumoured to fight with a rope around his neck, and a fellow privateer noted, "the desperate wretch must have been possessed by the devil." In clear violation of his parole, Johnson signed on as lieutenant under Captain William Dobson of *Young Teazer*.

Young Teazer was a more powerful successor to *Teazer*, armed with five guns, three of them wooden dummies intended to cow her victims into submission. On her first and only voyage, she captured a brig and a schooner off Sambro Light outside Halifax Harbour before escaping to hide in island-studded Mahone Bay on June 26, 1813.

The man-of-war *La Hogue* (74 guns), frigate *Orpheus* (32 guns) and privateer *Sir John Sherbrooke* were soon in pursuit, attempting to trap *Young Teazer* before she could slip out to sea under cover of darkness. When the bay grew too shallow for his warship, Captain the Honourable Thomas Bladen Capel lowered *La Hogue*'s five boats, each with a carronade mounted in her bow and laden with armed sailors. As the boats closed in on the American privateer that night and her crew debated their ever-decreasing options, the devil in Johnson took over. He went to the galley, returned with a burning brand and a demented look on his face and strode forcefully towards the magazine where several hundred pounds of gunpowder were stored.

Although his intentions were obvious, no one tried to stop him. *Young Teazer* exploded in a geranium-coloured burst of flame that lit up the night sky and rocked the shores of Mahone Bay as far as 12 miles away. Her whole after part was blown to the heavens, but the rest of her hull continued to float for several hours. Twenty-eight of her crew died immediately. Only nine survived, two of them mangled painfully. Eight of the survivors were captured immediately, but somehow Dobson managed to get away to fight another day.

Locals towed the wrecked remains of *Young Teazer* to what is now Meisner's Island, where they salvaged more than 100 miscellaneous items that eventually found their way into nearby homes. Her hull timbers became the foundation of a building that eventually became a restaurant, and white oak from her keelson was fashioned into a chancel cross for St. Stephen's Church in Chester, where two of her crewmen are buried.

Young Teazer's greatest mark on the local community remains the "*Teazer* Light." According to folklore a single shimmer of light appears out of nowhere and follows the wake of the doomed ship across the bay in the dark of night. When it reaches the spot where the ship exploded, it expands into a dark red glare before disappearing suddenly.

A few weeks later, back in New York, Captain William Dobson received command of what was once *Liverpool Packet*, renamed *Young Teazer's Ghost*. He was unsuccessful during her lone voyage and failed to take even one prize. Her owners sold her and she returned to sea under Captain John Perkins as the privateer *Portsmouth Packet*, perhaps a play on her original Nova Scotian name. During her next voyage in October 1813, she sailed north towards the Bay of Fundy in search of prizes, only to be spotted off the coast of Maine by the British brig *Fantôme* and forced to strike her colours after a 13-hour chase.

Taken to Halifax and condemned by the Court of Vice-Admiralty, she was put up for auction for the third time in two years and was purchased by none other than Enos Collins and his partners for exactly the same price they had paid before. She was once again named *Liverpool Packet*, and Caleb Seely, previously master of the tiny privateer schooner *Star* of Saint John, became her new captain in November.

Although the New Brunswicker never matched Barss's record, during two cruises he captured at least 14 ships in less than a year. He may have taken even more, but some of the records for 1814 are missing. Seely retired from privateering before the war ended, married Collins's sister and followed in Collins's footsteps by becoming a Liverpool shipowner and merchant.

Lewis Knaut, a Liverpool seaman who had sailed on *Liverpool Packet* as a prize-master, replaced Seely and took the schooner on her last privateering voyage in October 1814. Potential prizes were quite scarce by then due to the Royal Navy's almost total blockade of the American coast, and Knaut captured only four ships in her last two months. Her fiftieth and final prize sent to auction was *Fair Trader*, captured on December 6, 1814.

By the time her career ended, *Liverpool Packet*'s record was enough to make her the most successful privateer of the war on either side, having earned more than $250,000 in prize money. She also burned, sank or released several other ships, making her total catch well over 100 vessels during her 22-month existence as a raider.

Collins benefitted the most from *Liverpool Packet*'s career, but he actually made more money from another aspect of privateering. He and his partner, Joseph Allison, purchased prize ships and cargoes at auction for rock-bottom prices and resold them at a considerable profit. He founded a merchant company and, with seven of Halifax's most powerful merchants and financiers—including his partner, Allison, and Samuel Cunard—went on to establish one of Canada's first banks in 1825. The Halifax Banking

Company, known locally as the Collins Bank, soon controlled most of the economic life of the province and enjoyed a profitable monopoly for seven years.

The original bank building still stands in Halifax's Historic Properties, Canada's oldest surviving group of waterfront warehouses. These include the Privateers' Warehouse, built in 1813, where authorities auctioned prizes and their cargoes.

Collins later moved into the political life of the colony, amassed a large fortune through banking and other investments and built a fine estate, Gorsebrook, now the site of Saint Mary's University. When he died in 1871 at the age of 97, he was reputedly the richest man in British North America, leaving an estate valued at $6,000,000.

Collins was not Liverpool's only successful privateer. Thomas Freeman began his career in 1799, sailing against French and Spanish ships plying the waters of the West Indies. Over the years, he had been captured, freed, press-ganged and listed as dead. Yet, he remained a privateer, supplementing his income by carrying regular cargo between various ports during his many voyages. He participated in the very first act of war at sea after U.S. President Madison's declaration.

In the summer of 1812, Freeman and his crew were homeward bound from the West Indies when the large American frigate *Constitution* (44 guns) captured them and their ship; it was a harsh way to find out that the United States had declared war against Great Britain only days earlier. Imprisoned below deck, Freeman and his men cruised for weeks as *Constitution* sought additional victims. Then, on August 19, she found one.

Out of sight of the prisoners, a great sea battle raged. When it was all over, more prisoners joined the Liverpool privateers— bleeding, wounded and crippled sailors and marines from the Halifax-based *Guerrière*. Freeman and his mates could not believe their eyes and ears—a Royal Navy frigate taken and her crew in chains. Thomas Freeman resolved to do something about it.

After being released, the 37-year-old Freeman made one cruise in Collins's *Liverpool Packet* in December 1812, earning enough money for him and his partner, Snow Parker, to buy a ship. For £530, they purchased the Salem privateer *Revenge*, formerly *John and George*, taken by the British man-of-war schooner *Paz* off the Jeddore Ledges. Revenge was what Freeman had in mind, but he changed her name to *Retaliation*, a more subtle expression of his intentions.

At 71 tons and 60 feet long, she was only slightly larger than *Liverpool Packet*, and mounted two 4-pounders and a long 12-pounder on a pivot. Freeman added a pair of 12-pound carronades, no doubt relishing the thought of turning both American and British guns against American ships. With 50 men and a privateer's commission dated February 10, 1813, *Retaliation* sailed for the New England shore in the first week of March.

Success came quickly. Off Cape Cod on March 11, Freeman took the large sloop *Hunter* with a cargo of corn and staves; the next day the schooner *William* became his captive. Sailing in company with *Liverpool Packet* and *Sir John Sherbrooke*, *Retaliation* seized three sloops, followed on March 19 by the seizure of the schooner *Three Friends* and the brig *Victory*. They then drove the schooner *Betsy* ashore. Two days later, Freeman chased the schooner *Zenith* onto the rocks and took yet another. After so many captures, his small hold was laden with prisoners. Perhaps remembering his dark days when he shared a similar fate, he put them ashore and headed for home.

In two weeks, Freeman had taken possession of prizes worth $30,000; his small investment had returned more than he had made in 20 years at sea. He was anxious to go back to the New England coast, but those 20 years, some of them spent under the worst of conditions, had been hard. His health was failing. Although he would no longer go to sea as a privateer's commander, he and his partner, Parker, as *Retaliation*'s owners, continued to enjoy the benefits brought by ownership of a successful privateer.

During the war, Nova Scotia also sent authorized privateers to sea from Annapolis Royal (*Matilda* and *Broke*), Windsor (*Retrieve*) and Lunenburg (*Lunenburg*). Captain John Burkett Jr. and his 40-man crew drawn from Annapolis Royal, Granville and Digby took the five-gun, 50-ton *Matilda* along the Maine coast, capturing 13 prizes in three months over the course of three cruises. Many of the prizes were small coasters or fishing vessels. Burkett was practicing, as one historian noted, "privateering with a fine-tooth comb." Surprisingly, the Court of Vice-Admiralty condemned them all, despite frequent admonitions to privateers not to molest simple fishermen, advice most privateers followed, particularly the best.

In one of the war's more bizarre privateering incidents, *Matilda* captured *Loyal Sam*, a 280-ton former British merchantman, originally bound from the Bahamas to Scotland with a mixed cargo.

When Burkett's sailors stormed *Loyal Sam* at dusk, they discovered that the men they were fighting were from *Sir John Sherbrooke*, another Nova Scotia privateer whose crew had swarmed aboard at the same time from the other side of the vessel. The Court of Vice-Admiralty ruled a joint recapture. Normally recaptures were not worth very much, but in this instance the prize court awarded one-sixth of the appraised value of the ship and her cargo. The two privateers shared £9,424 in prize money. Sometime later, the Americans captured *Matilda* and in July 1814 sent her to Halifax under a flag of truce with English prisoners from Salem.

Annapolis Royal's second privateer during the war, the 50-foot-long schooner *Broke*, was the former American raider *Juliana Smith*, captured by the Royal Navy's *Nymph* in May 1813. Phineas Lovett, an Annapolis Royal merchant, purchased her at auction; she sailed in July, fitted out with four 12-pound carronades, a long 9-pounder, and a relatively small 35-man crew under Daniel Wade. Wade took 17 prizes that summer, many of them in full view—and range—of American shore batteries.

On August 4, *Broke* chased the sloop *Freeport* until she was brought to by shots from the privateer off Portland, Maine. As a prize crew rowed over, American cannons from a fort within half a mile blazed away at them. One of the boarding crew believed the sloop was bound for Portland, but with batteries firing on them the privateers had no time to question the sloop's crew. The prize crew managed to get the American boat out of the bay without being sunk, covered all the while by fire from *Broke's* guns.

Sometimes greed overcame any natural cautiousness that lightly armed privateer captains may have had. The 50-ton schooner *Fly* sailed from Halifax under Enoch Stanwood, who co-owned *Fly* with Israel Harding and Charles Hill. Stanwood took his first prize on June 17, 1813, three weeks after receiving his privateer's commission. Finding an American sloop at anchor in a Massachusetts harbour, he made toward her, but she weighed anchor and headed farther up the harbour to safety—or so her crew thought.

Fly buzzed after her, five shots from her one 9-pounder and two 6-pounders quickly forcing the intended victim to stop. Stanwood had captured the sloop *Packet* of Salem, carrying a cargo of wood and dried fish, right in front of the Massachusetts militia, which was firing its muskets without effect at the raider. Ironically, the American privateer *Fame* shortly recaptured *Packet*, only to be taken in turn by Annapolis Royal's *Matilda*.

Stanwood disappears from the historical record at this juncture, to be replaced as *Fly*'s captain by Elkanah Clements Jr. in July. Clements continued to raid, as Stanwood had, along the New England coast, capturing five prizes in as many days on his first cruise and sending them to Yarmouth. Shortly afterwards, the American brig-of-war *Enterprise* sighted Clements in the company of his latest prize, the sloop *Dolphin*, and gave chase. *Dolphin* got away, but unbelievably, *Fly* could not resist the temptation to stop and take another prize, the large brig *Diamond*, laden with $20,000 worth of molasses. It proved to be her undoing, as *Enterprise* caught up with and captured her. Both *Dolphin* and *Diamond* made Halifax safely.

While Liverpool sent the most privateers to sea, the brig *Sir John Sherbrooke* of Halifax may have been the finest privateer in the Maritimes. At 278 tons, she was certainly the largest, mounting 18 guns and carrying a crew of 150, including 50 sailors to act as marines. Although she sailed from the colony's capital, she was largely backed by Liverpool money. Commissioned as a raider in February 1813, *Sherbrooke* was the former American privateer *Thorn*, which had been captured by the British frigate *Tenedos* in 1812, then condemned and bought by the enterprising Liverpool trio of Knaut and the Barss Brothers. Her other owners were Enos Collins and Joseph Allison of Halifax, plus Joseph Freeman of Liverpool. Freeman, an older brother of Thomas Freeman of *Retaliation*, was also her captain.

For Freeman, a militia colonel, his actions during the War of 1812 constituted his second stint leading a privateer. He had commanded three other privateers a decade earlier in the war against France and Spain. One of them was *Charles Mary Wentworth*, on which both Enos Collins and Joseph Barss Jr. had shipped. Freeman brought a sense of discipline to his ship: she was run more like a Royal Navy vessel than a privateer. Although *Sherbrooke*'s career was short, it was glorious, with nearly a score of prizes within three months.

Freeman sailed on his first cruise in mid-March 1813, hunting the lucrative American coastal trade off Massachusetts. *Sherbrooke* captured 14 prizes on the voyage, carrying such varied cargoes as salt, beef, pork, gin, rum, brandy, tobacco and leather. The next month, Freeman was back again, this time in company with two Royal Navy ships, a task for which he was eminently suited. Although the warships took 11 prizes, none of them were shared with *Sherbrooke*'s crew.

Freeman took only four more prizes on other voyages that spring, as fewer and fewer American ships broke through the British blockade into open water. This turn of events had a direct effect on *Sherbrooke*'s fate, and her owners sold her in August 1813. Her new owners converted her into an armed merchantman, plying the routes to Europe and the West Indies.

On a voyage to Spain carrying a cargo of fish, *Sherbrooke* was captured by the American privateer *Syren*. The British blockade that had driven *Sherbrooke* from privateering prevented the American ship from bringing her home, so her captors burned her. Joseph Freeman's post-privateering career was much more distinguished than that of his former ship: he became a member of the provincial legislature.

A letter of marque was no guarantee of success. The schooner *Rolla* of Liverpool was a 132-ton, 80-foot-long former American privateer of the same name, captured by the Royal Navy's *Loire* on December 10, 1813. Several well-known Liverpool privateer owners had shares in *Rolla*, among them Joseph Freeman, the Barss Brothers, Benjamin Knaut, Enos Collins and his partner, Joseph Allison. Mounting a long 18-pounder and four carronades, she sailed profitably for six months after receiving her letter of marque in June 1814, sending a number of prizes home. In January 1815, under Joseph Bartlett, she sailed on her last cruise, carrying 45 of Liverpool's most experienced privateers, 15 of whom had already served as captains.

The privateers did not know it but the war was already over. Although the peace treaty had been signed on Christmas Eve, word did not reach Nova Scotia for over two months. On January 13, *Rolla* sighted the schooner *Comet*, gave chase and caught her off Martha's Vineyard after nine hours. Putting a three-man prize crew aboard, Bartlett sent *Comet* to Liverpool while he headed off in search of more victims. That night a furious storm hit, but *Comet* rode it out and reached Liverpool a week later.

During the next few days, no more prizes from *Rolla* reached her homeport. Days became weeks, weeks became months, and still nothing was heard from the schooner. If *Rolla* and her crew had been captured, word would have been received that they were prisoners. In fact, with the war over, they would have certainly been exchanged. Their relatives could only assume the worst—*Rolla* had been lost with all 42 hands, as well as nine prisoners taken off *Comet*.

If that were the case, 22 Liverpool wives were widowed, and more than 100 children orphaned. Among the missing was John Freeman, *Liverpool Packet*'s first captain, who had been making his third cruise on *Rolla*. Still, some wives held out hope that their husbands would one day return, including Freeman's wife, who lived to be 90. Small wonder that widow's walks are such a common architectural feature of houses along the South Shore. Finally, in 1820, a great gale washed a waterlogged wreck onto the beach of Essex County, Massachusetts. It had been so long under the sea that it hardly resembled a ship anymore. On a broken plank, the letters "R O L L " and part of the letter "A" were carved. The mystery of *Rolla*'s fate was finally solved.

The last maritime privateer commissioned for the war was the Liverpool schooner *Dove*. She received her letter of marque on January 24, 1815, exactly one month after the peace treaty had been signed. At 30 tons and with a crew of 20, she mounted a 4-pounder and four swivels. Under James Harrington she took two prizes off Massachusetts in February, the pinky *Atlas* and the brig *George*. Although both ships had been seized after the war officially ended, under the terms of the peace treaty they were held to be lawful prizes. *George* was the last prize of the war.

3

PRISON ISLAND

"This day we embark'd for Hell."

The May 2, 1814, journal entry of captured Connecticut privateer Benjamin Franklin Palmer reflected his despair as he entered the British prison at Melville Island on the western side of Halifax's Northwest Arm. A crewman on the privateer *Rolla*, he had been captured by the Royal Navy off New York's Long Island on December 10, 1813. He lived with 200 fellow prisoners in an extremely confined space; their only pastime was gambling as they waited in hope for parole or exchange. Occasionally the prisoners had an unpleasant task to attend to: a fellow inmate would die and a burial party would be formed to lay the man to rest on nearby Deadman's Island.

May 2 was not an unusual day on Melville Island. Consisting of four acres of land near the head of the Northwest Arm, the island became a place of suffering for much of its post-contact history. Together with nearby Deadman's Island, a swampy spit surmounted by a piney knoll just over two acres in size, Melville Island would see many deaths and burials besides those of Americans captured during the War of 1812. French and Spanish prisoners as well as black refugees would all find themselves confined—in one way or another—to these two tiny islands.

Melville Island was one of the earliest prisons constructed by the British specifically to handle prisoners of war after Revolutionary France declared war on Britain in January 1793. Before that time there was no formal method for dealing with them. Although the Treaty of Amiens brought a brief respite from hostilities, war broke out again in May 1803.

Shortly afterwards, on July 9, French prisoners arrived in Halifax and Vice Admiral Sir Andrew Mitchell, commanding the North American Squadron, asked Lieutenant-Governor Sir John Wentworth to accept them. Wentworth refused, stating they were the navy's responsibility. Without any suitable location in which to hold the prisoners, Mitchell was forced to send them to England.

Later that summer, the first French prisoners were brought to the island, which was at that time named after its owner, fish merchant James Kavanagh. The British initially housed them in Kavanagh's former home and outbuildings. On August 24, a detachment of one sergeant and five privates from the 29th Regiment, plus two corporals and four privates from the 60th Regiment, mounted the island's first guard over the prisoners. Three weeks later a subaltern, corporal, drummer and ten privates reinforced the guard, with further soldiers added as the prison's population increased. Eventually, a full company would be required to carry out the duty.

A year after the army mounted the first guard, Captain Robert Murray purchased the island and part of the nearby mainland on behalf of the Royal Navy for £1,000, a handsome return for Kavanagh on his original £65 investment nearly 20 years earlier. Either Kavanagh was an exceptionally sharp trader or a state of almost continuous war had driven up prices. Murray had arrived in Halifax the previous December as "Agent to the Commissioners for conducting His Majesty's Transport Service and for the care and custody of Prisoners of war."

The navy promptly renamed the island after the new First Lord of the Admiralty, Viscount Melville, but the army continued to provide the guards. By 1808, Kavanagh's old buildings were much the worse for wear and the guards and inmates were suffering through the severe winters. So the navy built new quarters—a large wooden prison and a house on the island's hill to serve as the prison governor's residence.

Between 1803 and Napoleon's final defeat at Waterloo in June 1815, the British incarcerated more French prisoners at Melville Island. A total of 75 of the Emperor's men perished, there including nine Spanish prisoners. The British did not transfer all the French prisoners first brought to Halifax to Melville Island. They transferred some to Britain and placed others on parole.

We owe the first known description of the prison to a French sailor, François Lambert Bourneuf. Bourneuf spent three years on Melville after he was captured on the French frigate *Furieuse* in 1809. He arrived the year after the navy built the new wooden prison. In 1812 he managed to escape but he remained in the

François Lambert Bourneuf, a French sailor captured by the British, was sent to the prison on Halifax's Melville Island in 1809.

colony, married and had several successful occupations. In later
life, he wrote an account of his time in prison.

Bourneuf started writing in 1859, half a century after he had been
taken prisoner, and time may have clouded his memory, as several
of his descriptions of prison life border on the idyllic. Then again,
he may have decided to show his adopted country in the best light:

> *Melville Prison is on a little island that covers twenty acres*
> [actually four]. *A bridge on the south side connects the*
> *island to the mainland, and a boat on the east side brings*
> *all of the provisions, the soldiers, and many of the visitors.*
> *The prison itself was on the west side of the island. It was*
> *about three hundred feet long, eighty feet wide, and thir-*
> *ty feet high. The hospital, the jailer's quarters, and the*
> *interpreter's lodging were upstairs . . . . The prison was*
> *divided lengthwise into three parts. In the centre was a*
> *common area for prisoners, for walking, for setting up*
> *their shops and counters, and for the dancing masters*
> [instructors] *to exercise. At night, there was a place to put*
> *large tubs that contained our necessities. Men hired by the*
> *government removed these tubs . . . . They took the*
> *garbage to the harbour through a large door intended for*
> *this purpose. There was also a place to wash our feet*
> *. . . . The other parts were divided every eight feet into*
> *"ports," each of which housed thirty inmates. In each port,*
> *there were posts that reached the ceiling, and between the*
> *posts were cross-pieces, about six feet apart, to which we*
> *attached our hammocks. There also were smaller cross-*
> *pieces that served as ladders to our hammocks. Those who*
> *slept higher up risked breaking their necks, but they got*
> *used to it . . . . The prison yard was enclosed by pointed*
> *stakes that were twelve to fifteen feet high and that were*
> *supported by cross-pieces . . . . Along the posts in the low-*
> *est areas were four outhouses that the sea cleaned at high*
> *tide. On the other side were the guards' barracks, the mag-*
> *azines, and the officers' lovely house.*

Bourneuf described the prison as a healthy place, where he never saw a serious illness among the prisoners. The hospital, located on the western side of the island, provided bedspace for 100, although Bourneuf claimed he never saw it full. Given that there were only 75 deaths among the French and the Spanish over a 12-year period, his memory here rings true.

Many inmates went to the hospital simply to get a quart of wine, which was provided to patients for the nominal sum of five pence. The Halifax doctor who treated the men knew the system was being abused, but he let the men have the wine unless they became drunk and caused a nuisance. According to Bourneuf, very few deaths occurred, and the guards buried those who died in the cemetery across the bridge.

Bourneuf's diary also provides the first account of daily life at the prison. The prisoners filled their time by making clothing, implements and trinkets, which they sold at a thriving bazaar; goods included stockings, mitts, gloves, purses, birchbark hats, bone snuff boxes, knives, forks, dice, dominoes and even model ships. Bourneuf possessed no particular handicraft skills when he arrived at the prison, but he soon learned a few by observing his fellow prisoners. He began by knitting woollen gloves. Next, he noticed that items made from bone sold for far more than anything else, so he quickly learned how to work with bone.

Sailors and soldiers visited the prison on weekdays to view and buy goods. Townspeople came on Sundays. The prison resembled a small town fair, even including lotteries and games of chance, with crafts for prizes. Sometimes the prisoners took in more than £100 a day, which would usually be divided among more than 500 inmates.

The prison staff provided a large pot in the kitchen to heat water so that prisoners could wash themselves and their clothes; in winter, the staff set up two large stoves in the barracks to keep prisoners warm. The inmates carried their own water over the bridge from the mainland, accompanied by armed guards. Bourneuf noted the inmates had all the fish they needed, as they could fish for themselves through the space between the posts surrounding the island, or buy fish from the local fishermen who came to sell their catch. The prisoners cleaned the fish at the same spot where they washed their feet. Bourneuf described the feeding arrangements in detail:

> *Our soup was cooked in two large pots. In addition, we each received half a pound of meat per day, which was weighed by the butcher. The inmates were divided into groups of seven, and each group had an eighteen-inch-long spit with string. When it was done, the cook, paid eight dollars a month, took a long iron fork and put it into wooden tubs. Then he rang a bell, and each prisoner approached with his wooden bowl. Using a large copper ladle, the cook gave each inmate a spoonful of broth and his ration of meat. We received our supplies of meat, bread, potatoes, and salt every second day.*

The inmates chose two different prisoners each day to cut the meat. If they found the meat or bread unacceptable, which frequently happened, they made the butcher or the baker bring in better supplies. "A few times, the meat looked like a drowned dog, and the bread could have stuck to a wall," Bourneuf observed. He knew it was not the authorities' fault, but the contractor's. After the prisoners complained, the suppliers brought better rations, but the inmates often went without food for up to two days. If they had not taken action, the contractor would have brought worse and worse food. The prisoners knew they held the advantage: if they refused the supplies, commissioners would be appointed to investigate.

At first, the British extended leniency towards their French prisoners. They placed officers on parole and allowed the men to leave the island and roam freely or work in Halifax, if they pledged not to escape. When some of them failed to keep their promise, local residents felt particularly galled, as a number of Haligonians were suffering in French prisons at the time.

Prisoners tried to escape whenever an opportunity arose, but few succeeded. Some slipped away during blizzards, making good their escape over the ice-covered Northwest Arm. Some undoubtedly perished by falling through the ice. Guards put recaptured escapees into solitary confinement cells in the "black hole" in the prison's cellar, and fed them bread and water. In admiration, the other prisoners generously shared their rations with escapees thrown into the hole. Some of the prisoners who did get away, including Bourneuf, remained in the colony and married local women. Bourneuf escaped and was recaptured twice before he got away for good, becoming the best-known successful escapee from the island.

After several prisoners broke their parole, the British imposed restrictions. To help prevent escapes, the prison always had five or six guards on duty. They counted the prisoners every morning and evening, counting a second time if the tally came out wrong. The governor severely punished soldiers who allowed prisoners to get away, as well as any inmates discovered to have helped in the escape.

The British allowed French prisoners to work on road crews, supervised by overseers, in order to improve the colony's roads. The inmates enjoyed such work for two reasons: it helped alleviate the interminable boredom of prison life and, even more importantly, it provided the best opportunity for escape. While working as a member of a 20-man road crew near Truro, Bourneuf ran away with two other prisoners one night. The guards recaptured them the next night and marched them back to Melville Island. The three escapees were put in the black hole on bread and water for ten days.

In 1812, Bourneuf received permission to join another work crew repairing the Prospect Road. After three months, he and some companions stole a small sailboat and headed out to sea, hoping to run into an American privateer. They sailed along the South Shore, making landfall at Port l'Hébert, but were captured by locals and put into the Shelburne jail.

Bourneuf escaped for the final time when the authorities loaded him onto a boat to go back to Halifax. He eventually settled on St. Mary's Bay where he became in succession a schoolteacher, seaman, shipbuilder and finally Member of the Legislative Assembly from 1843 to 1859, the year in which he began to write his account of life on Melville Island.

Just as the British did not have a system in place in 1793 for dealing with prisoners of war, the Americans had no such system when the War of 1812 broke out. With so many prisoners being captured, they were soon forced to design one. Initially, marshals in each state were responsible for them; eventually they reported to a Commissary General for Prisoners, a new position established by the government.

Both the British and the American opponents appointed agents to look out for prisoners' welfare in each other's countries. Thomas Barclay, a Nova Scotia Loyalist from the Annapolis Valley, became the British agent in November 1812, taking up his post in New York in April 1813. The Americans stationed an agent in Britain and another one at Halifax. John Mitchell, a diplomat, came to the city in October 1812.

The agents' responsibilities included ensuring the prisoners were properly fed and clothed, treated when sick, parolled appropriately and paid a weekly allowance. Mitchell's duties also comprised arranging prisoner exchanges, an important responsibility, as Halifax soon became a major centre for these transfers. The prison at Melville Island was becoming even more crowded with the arrival of American prisoners, and the British were anxious to exchange them for their own captured men. Initially, both sides had a generous policy on exchanges and quickly sent prisoners, mainly privateers during the first few months of the war, home on parole.

Government agents in Halifax representing both Britain and the United States developed a key document relating to prisoners captured during the War of 1812. It is a remarkable work, reflecting a concern for the proper care and treatment of prisoners of war long before the Hague Convention of 1907 or the Geneva Conventions of 1929 and 1949 even started to address this issue. The British in particular wanted an agreement for the formal exchange of prisoners: large numbers of parolled British soldiers and sailors were roaming the streets of Halifax unable to participate in the fighting.

Under the parole system, these men could not rejoin their forces to fight again until official, confirmed lists of prisoners were first exchanged between the two sides. Once this occurred, those on the

The prison buildings on Melville Island as seen from Halifax, across the Northwest Arm, c. 1818.

lists were free from their parole and were legally permitted to take up arms. The British urged Mitchell to negotiate such an agreement, using a system of equivalencies for each rank.

The ultimate local authority for any prisoners taken by the Royal Navy was Vice Admiral Sir John Borlase Warren, commander of the Royal Navy's North American Station at Halifax. He worked closely with the lieutenant-governor on the handling and disposition of prisoners. Warren selected Richard John Uniacke, the province's attorney general and advocate general, and Royal Navy Lieutenant William Miller, Agent for Prisoners of War, to represent Britain's interests in negotiations with Mitchell.

On November 28, 1812, the three reached a provisional agreement entitled "Cartel for the Exchange of Prisoners of War between Great Britain and the United States of America," and submitted it to the American and British authorities for ratification by their respective governments. President Madison apparently wanted a few changes made before he would agree to the terms of the document and no further action was taken. As a result, a final approved agreement was never signed, although both sides generally adhered to its terms during the war.

In 15 articles, the cartel outlined the responsibilities both countries held for those captured in battle. The first article decreed that prisoners were to be treated with the same humanity exercised by civilized nations during war and should be exchanged as speedily as circumstances permitted. It then established that equal ranks could be exchanged either for each other or for a certain number of men, based on an established exchange rate. All ranks were covered, from admirals or generals (each worth 60 men), through naval captains or colonels (fifteen men) and petty officers or non-commissioned officers (two men), down to seamen and private soldiers, who were exchanged one for one.

Article two defined non-combatants, such as surgeons, chaplains, ships' passengers, men not in the services, boys under 12 and women and girls. It exempted them from capture or imprisonment and directed their immediate release if taken. The third article named the cities where prisoners could be exchanged and permitted each nation to station an agent near these locations to inspect the management and care of the prisoners of war. Halifax and Quebec were the only such locations in British North America. This article also allowed agents to reside near non-exchange depots, in order to monitor and inspect the prisoners' care.

The next three articles dealt with various aspects of parole. Article four described the documentary form of the parole, including the geographic limits, hours and other rules to be observed. It also established what allowance parolees would receive from the agents, to be doubled in cases of sickness. Parolees who disobeyed the rules could be sent back to prison.

Article five concerned prisoners returned to their native countries to serve their parole. Such prisoners had to promise not to serve again until duly exchanged and to sign an undertaking to that effect. Article six noted that prisoners who violated their parole "shall be liable to be dealt with according to the usages and customs observed in such cases by the most civilized nations when at war." This included the right of the paroling nation to demand the return of any prisoners who broke their parole in their own countries.

The seventh article stated that no prisoner could be struck with a hand, whip, stick, or any other weapon and that prisoners were entitled to have their complaints and grievances resolved. If prisoners became disorderly, they could be closely confined and kept on two-thirds rations for up to ten days. Prisoners were to be provided with "a subsistence of sound and wholesome provisions," consisting of a pound of beef or twelve ounces of pork, a pound of wheaten bread and a quarter of a pint of peas or six ounces of rice or a pound of potatoes per man per day. Two quarts of salt and four quarts of vinegar were for every 100 days of rations.

Agents could approve other choices of meat and vegetables, as long as they were of "equal nutriment," but could not change the ratio of meat to vegetables. Agents could also provide clothing and a small allowance to prisoners, as well as inspect the quality and quantity of rations at any time.

The next seven articles dealt with the exchange of prisoners. Article eight provided for each side to expedite exchanges as far as circumstances permitted and to only hold back prisoners for good and sufficient cause. Article nine allocated two cartel vessels from each nation, preferably of 500 tons but not less than 200 tons, to be employed in a regular exchange of prisoners; it went on to detail arrangements for guards, flags of truce, provisions and other matters. The tenth article covered procedures for the transportation of prisoners prior to the establishment of regular cartels, as well as those for temporary cartels.

Article eleven permitted commanders of warships to deliver prisoners of war under a flag of truce to any established exchange station, while article twelve allowed commanders of warships or privateers to send prisoners to such stations in neutral vessels. In both instances, all prisoners delivered by these methods were to be properly receipted and credited to the sending nation.

The thirteenth article concerned confirmed lists of exchanged prisoners. Once agents exchanged such documents, those on the list were to be considered as liberated and free to serve again. Article fourteen covered the possibility of one side sending more prisoners for exchange than it received in return. In such a case, that country could stop sending additional prisoners until the numbers were equal.

The fifteenth and final article concerned ratification of the agreement. During the war, the British sent thousands of captured American sailors, privateers and soldiers to Melville Island. The General Entry Book, detailing names, capture and disposition, shows 8,148 imprisoned there over the course of the war. Many of the American soldiers were taken at the battles of the Niagara Peninsula, but most prisoners were captured on the high seas, including the crews of at least 40 privateers and merchantmen, as well as the crews of various warships, such as *Chesapeake*.

The British had particular concerns about the exchange of privateers. At their insistence, the agreement only permitted captains, lieutenants and mates of privateers to be exchanged. It was a ploy intended to discourage privateering, but it had little effect. American privateers rushed into British and international waters as soon as Madison declared war, and were not deterred when the British captured 24 of their ships during the first two months of the war.

Despite the fact that privateers eligible for exchange were to be considered on the same basis as other prisoners, many remained imprisoned much longer than normal, or were sent to England's dreaded Dartmoor Prison for the remainder of the war in an attempt to discourage privateering.

Dartmoor Prison was constructed in 1806–09 for French prisoners, but later held American ones. Situated on bleak, desolate and sparsely populated moorland in the wild upland country of the county of Devon in southwest England, it soon developed a reputation as the most infamous of all British prisons because of the brutal mistreatment prisoners received there.

Perez Drinkwater of North Yarmouth, Maine, sailed as lieutenant on the privateer *Lucy* when a British brig captured him in late 1813. Landed at Plymouth, England, he and his fellow prisoners were marched through a February snowstorm to Dartmoor, where they found about 10,000 other inmates.

Drinkwater fervently hoped he would get out before the war ended so he could "have the pleasure of killing one Englishman and drinking his blood," as he regarded the British as the worst of all the human race. He called Dartmoor "one of the most retched [places] in this habbited world" and was afflicted by bedbugs and lice. He estimated that every prisoner was host to at least 1,000 of these vermin.

Shipping prisoners to England did not entirely solve the problem of overcrowding. By September, the navy had a thousand prisoners at Melville Island. To alleviate the immediate strain, a condemned prize from the Court of Vice-Admiralty was purchased and anchored off the island to hold some of them. The use of old, rotting, unseaworthy ships to hold prisoners was common during the Wars of the French Revolution and the Napoleonic Wars. They were referred to as "prison hulks."

One of the first descriptions of such hulks occurs in Charles Dickens's novel *Great Expectations*. Abel Magwitch, a convicted criminal, was sentenced to 14 years on the "Medway Hulks," anchored near the mouth of the Thames River in England. Pip, the narrator of the story, describes Magwitch's floating prison as "a black-hulk lying out a little way from the mud of the shore, like a wicked Noah's ark. Cribbed and barred and moored by massive rusty chains, the prison-ship seemed in my young eyes to be ironed like the prisoners." Confined below decks in cramped, musty, damp surroundings, life for the inmates unfortunate enough to be condemned to a prison hulk was one of daily misery.

Dr. Amos Babcock sailed as assistant surgeon on a small Salem privateer, mounting four carriage guns and a crew of 90, on January 5, 1813. He had "no other ideas than that of a pleasant cruise, and making a fortune." He was soon disabused of both notions. On May 20, the frigate *Tenedos*, under Captain Hyde Parker, captured Babcock's ship off Martha's Vineyard. *Tenedos* had been sent off on an independent mission by Captain Broke of *Shannon* as he tried to draw *Chesapeake* out of Boston. After repeated broadsides from the British warship, the privateer struck her colours.

Parker immediately transferred the captured Americans to the
brig *Curlew*, commanded by Halifax native Lieutenant Head.
When the prisoners arrived in Halifax on May 29, soldiers formed
them up and marched them through the streets, "so as to make as
grand a show as possible," in Babcock's opinion. The guards
marched them to a landing and took them by boat across the
Northwest Arm to Melville Island. At the gate, prison staff issued
hammocks and blankets, called the roll and then ordered the captured Americans into the prison yard.

Lieutenant William Miller, who helped negotiate the exchange
agreement, acted as British agent for the prisoners and ran Melville
Island. When new prisoners arrived, prison staff separated the
Americans and French, and the whites and blacks before assigning
them to combined living and eating areas known as messes.

Babcock found it all very discouraging, and his description of
the prison and its activities is in stark contrast to Bourneuf's,
although little had actually changed by the time American prisoners began to arrive. "I shall never forget the first impression,
which the sight of my wretched looking countrymen made on my
feelings. Here we were, at once, surrounded by a ragged set of
quidnuncs [gossips], eagerly inquiring *What news?*—where were we

This 34-cell addition to the Melville Island prison was built in 1884.

taken? and how? and what success we had met with before we were taken?"

Babcock noticed the various tasks in which the prisoners were engaged. Some were washing their clothes. Others mended them. Still others were intent on ridding their shirts and other clothing from lice—much to the disgrace of the British government, in Babcock's opinion.

He went on to describe the prison layout in detail:

> The buildings on Melville Island are constructed of wood. Beside the prison, there is a cooking house, barracks for soldiers, and a storehouse; a house for the officers, and another for the surgeon. There are a couple of cannon pointing towards the prison, and a Telegraph, for the purpose of giving intelligence to the fort, which overlooks the island and the town of Halifax. These buildings are painted red, and have upon the whole a neat appearance. The prison itself is two hundred feet in length and fifty in breadth. It is two stories high; the upper one is for officers, and the infirmary and dispensary; while the lower part is divided into two prisons, one for the French, the other for the Americans: the prison yard is little more than an acre—the whole island being little more than five acres. It is connected on the south side with the main land by a bridge. The parade, so called, is between the turnkey's [jailer's] house and the barracks. From all which it may be gathered that Melville Island is a very humble garrison, and a very dreary spot for the person who commands there.

He described the view from the prison as a range of dreary hills, which contained a few scattered buildings, attempts at farming, piles of rocks and bushes. "This unfruitful country is rightly named *New Scotland*. Barren and unfruitful as Old Scotland is, our *Nova Scotia* is worse." Babcock felt Melville Island suffered badly in comparison with American prisons. He noted that the prison building resembled a horse stable, with stalls for separating the animals from each other, above which hammocks hung in four tiers.

It was not so much the dullness of the surroundings as the disease-ridden state of the prison that affected many prisoners. Cramping and unsanitary conditions led to outbreaks of infectious diseases. Typhus, smallpox, dysentery, pneumonia and tuberculosis took a steady toll on the prisoners in their weakened state. Others simply succumbed to their wounds.

Babcock found about 900 fellow Americans in the prison, although many died due to the severity of the winter. He considered that the British government provided insufficient fuel to heat the prison.

His first night was not a pleasant experience. "The first time I was shut up for the night, in the prison, it distressed me too much to close my eyes. Its closeness and smell were disagreeable, but this was trifling to what I experienced afterwards, in another place. The general hum and confined noise from almost every hammock was at first, very distressing." After being locked up for the night like animals, the prisoners were woken by their guards the next morning. The grinding noise of the locks and the unbarring of the doors were accompanied by a cry of "turn out—all out."

After rising in the morning the prisoners lashed up their hammocks, carried them into the prison yard and formed for roll call. Some prisoners opened the windows while others carried out the "piss tubs," dumped the previous night's deposits and washed them out. This was the same procedure that British soldiers in barracks followed.

After rinsing out the tubs, the soldiers used them for personal washing, until army doctors decided that this practice caused eye infections and stopped it. The prisoners at Melville Island probably used the tubs to wash themselves as well, appointing their own inspectors to check the tubs for cleanliness.

Meanwhile, cooks from each of the messes went to the kitchen to brew coffee supplied by the American agent, John Mitchell. In addition, he provided sugar, extra potatoes and tobacco. Prisoners could also buy extra food, such as apples, smoked herring, lobsters, candy and spruce beer. Some enterprising inmates even ran canteens.

Miller was a stickler for cleanliness and made prisoners sweep out their building twice a week, each mess taking it in turn. On the days the prisoners washed the floors, Miller kept them waiting outside until the floors dried. Babcock considered this practice very distressing and dangerous to health, especially in rain and snow, as there was no place to take shelter. He believed it was simply a pretext to annoy them: the water turned to ice as soon as it hit the floors.

Miller, a strict disciplinarian, sent those who broke the rules to the same hole under the prison building where recaptured escapees were held, and he put them on the same diet of water and bread for up to ten days. Palmer called him "stiff as a crow bar." Babcock thought Miller could have alleviated the prisoners' sufferings if he had wished to, while still doing his duty. But Miller, as well as the turnkey, named Grant, seemed to take delight in tormenting the Americans.

When the prisoners complained about the quality of some beef, Miller mounted a staircase and began haranguing them. "Hundreds of you, d—d scoundrels, have been to me begging and pleading that I would interpose my influence that you might be the first to be exchanged . . . and now you have the impudence to tell me to my face, that the King's beef is not good enough for your dainty stomach . . . . You are a set of rascals . . . . You complain of ill treatment, when you have never faced better in your lives." He went on, pointing to a pile of lumber in the prison yard, "and if you die, there are boards enough for to make you coffins, and [a] hundred and fifty acres of land to bury you in." Miller used the threat of Dartmoor to keep prisoners in line.

Not all the prisoners viewed Miller in a bad light, however. A letter to the *Acadian Reporter*, signed by 11 American prisoners, denied allegations that he was "cruel, fraudulent and bordering on barbarity."

Whatever their opinion of Miller, there was no doubt about the prisoners' feelings for their own agent, John Mitchell. When he vis-

ited the island, prisoners greeted him respectfully. He worked tire-
lessly on their behalf, especially in the provision of rations and
clothing. He kept the prisoners in touch with the outside world,
delivering letters and newspapers, bringing news and collecting letters. Benjamin Franklin Palmer called him "a fine old man."

In his role as agent for the American prisoners, Mitchell received
several letters from inmates and their relatives in the United States
asking for his help in obtaining their exchange. One such letter,
from 57-year-old James Wakefield, who had been at Melville
Island for four months, noted he had received information that the
greater part of his family was ill and in want of the necessities of
life. He himself was "reduced very low by bodily infirmities" and
was "at present very badly afflicted with the gravel [a urinary tract
disorder]." Wakefield hoped this short outline of his problems
would convince Mitchell to send him home in an exchange ship.
Mitchell received many similar requests and it is doubtful he
would have been able to grant Wakefield's.

In July 1814, captured American officers gave Mitchell a letter in
which they expressed their gratitude for his attempts "in endeav-
ouring as far as possible to ameliorate the distress always incident
to a State of imprisonment." They also alluded to their fears of
being transferred to Dartmoor, by particularly thanking him for his
efforts (though fruitless) to prevent a number of prisoners being
sent to England.

During the day, once any duties had been completed, the prisoners remained largely on their own until evening. Gambling, especially backgammon, and dancing to the fiddle were popular. Guards
punished any fighting among the prisoners with a trip to the hole.
Talk centred on the latest news of exchanges and the possibility of
being included in one. After being locked in for the night, conversa-
tion, storytelling and singing continued until the 9 pm signal gun.

Apparently, British soldiers assigned as guards at Melville Island
found the place as boring as the inmates did. A general court martial
tried Lieutenant Anthony Keogh of the 64th Regiment in July 1813.
The court found him guilty of drunkenness when in command of
the guards, and cashiered him.

Besides British rules and regulations, the prisoners also enforced discipline among themselves. They elected their own officials, known as presidents, moderators and judges, on a weekly basis. A few details of their duties and responsibilities are known. A president apparently had the authority to call a court to sit, presided over by a judge and jury, to hear cases in which prisoners accused others of crimes against their comrades.

One of the most common crimes was theft, for which the standard punishment was flogging. The lash was even administered to cooks caught skimming the fat off soup for their own use, with 18 lashes being the standard punishment. The sting of the lash was something many sailors had already experienced at the hands of their own officers.

Babcock noted that about 200 Frenchmen, who had been prisoners since 1803, remained in Halifax. Few of them actually stayed in the prison; most worked in the town or taught dancing, fencing or French to the townspeople. Some found employment as butchers and cooks or nurses in hospitals, and were favoured for their politeness, obedience and good humour. The British didn't find the Americans quite as charming. "Sunday being a leisure day among the men of business in Halifax and its vicinity, the old *refugees* [Loyalists] from the United States used to come round the prison to gratify their eyes . . . with the sight of what they called *rebels*."

In the summer of 1813, the British sent 425 additional American prisoners to Halifax, most of them soldiers captured in the battles of the Niagara Peninsula. Babcock noted their arrival: "We were one day not a little shocked by the arrival of a number of American soldiers who were entrapped and taken with Colonel *Boerstler*, in Upper Canada. They exhibited a picture of misery, woe and dispair [sic]." He and his companions felt sorry for these raw, inexperienced militiamen, taken at Beaver Dams on June 23, 1813, then sent to Quebec by road and river and crowded onto transports, "like negroes in a guinea ship," where several died. More prisoners followed, this time sailors. "Early in the month of July, we were not a little disturbed by the arrival of the crew of our ill omened, ill fated *Chesapeake*."

As the population of the prison increased, Babcock and his fellow inmates enjoyed a joke at the expense of the townspeople. In August, Haligonians were alarmed by a rumour that the prisoners on Melville Island planned to break out and seize the city. When the Americans learned of the rumour they pretended to conspire by talking in small groups while pointing about in different directions. Their ruse rattled the British. The army placed artillery facing the island, stationed additional troops there and even prepared to arm some of the citizens. Miller began promising the prisoners an exchange, although he would not disclose their destination.

In September, Lieutenant-Governor Sherbrooke complained to Lord Bathurst that he needed more troops to guard Melville Island's population, now at 1,624. Bathurst replied that no more troops could be sent, but that some prisoners would be brought to Britain in the spring of 1814. While the prison population continued to rise due to the influx of prisoners, for some reason no prisoner exchanges were being made at the time. The added pressure on the prison led Warren to begin sending prisoners to Britain as early as the autumn of 1813, using merchant ships to transport them. Babcock was among them. On September 1, Miller told him and about 100 others that they were going to be sent home and he had them hastily gather up their belongings. Only once aboard ship did the guards inform them their destination was England. Babcock eventually ended up in Dartmoor, along with thousands of other captured Americans.

American prisoners were kept at Dartmoor long after the war ended. Angered by their continued imprisonment and poor food, on April 15, 1815, they demonstrated and refused to back down when ordered to do so. The Prison Commandant, Captain Shortland, called out the troops, who advanced on the prisoners, bayonets fixed. The inmates stood firm, but when Shortland issued the order to charge, the Americans broke and ran for shelter as fast as they could.

Someone gave the order to shoot and the troops fired a full volley into the mad scramble of prisoners desperately trying to get inside the buildings. Repeated volleys witnessed by Babcock and

Drinkwater killed seven and wounded 60 prisoners. Legend has it that most of the soldiers deliberately fired into the air, which would explain the relatively low death toll among thousands of prisoners crowded together in a confined space.

These deaths brought the total of Americans and French who died at Dartmoor to about 1,500, the majority of them American seamen. They were buried in a field beyond the prison walls. As a result of the brutal treatment American prisoners received at Dartmoor, a joint Anglo-American commission investigated conditions at the prison after the war and awarded compensation to the families of those who had died there.

In the 1990s, an "American Cemetery Restoration Project" was begun by United States servicemen stationed in Britain, with the aim of restoring the long-neglected American graves and erecting a monument listing the names of all the American dead.

More prisoners were brought to Halifax in the winter of 1813–14, taxing Melville Island's resources even further. In the meantime, Sir George Prevost, Governor-in-Chief for Upper and Lower Canada, reached an agreement with his American counterparts on prisoner exchange. In June 1814, the authorities shipped to Salem all the prisoners whom Prevost had sent to Halifax, immediately reducing the island's population by 1,200.

When a prisoner died, the guards would bury him on Deadman's Island, then known as Target Hill. Benjamin Franklin Palmer's journal provides some of the earliest descriptions of prisoner burials in the area. Two of his diary entries refer to them. On May 26, 1814, he noted that two died that week; then on June 4, "4 prisoners caried [sic] to Target Hill this morning a place where they bury the Dead—I'm fearful a number of us will visit that place this Summer, if not shortly released." The guards normally rowed the dead across to the tiny spit, their bodies swathed in canvas shrouds, before depositing them in shallow graves. In later years, the effects of rain and sea erosion exposed human bones on the land and in the water.

The British maintained meticulous records of the prisoners they captured and those who died—better records than the Americans kept of their own men. Between August 10, 1812 and March 30, 1815, a total of 195 American prisoners died. Of these, 188 are believed to have been buried on Deadman's Island, the other seven in the cemetery at the naval base.

After the war, Melville Island was put to other uses. From April 1815 to May 1816, it housed black refugees, some of whom died and were buried there. In 1847, it housed a group of Irish immigrants stricken with smallpox. Thirty of them died and were also buried there. In 1856, Melville Island became a prison again. A fire destroyed the old wooden prison in 1935.

In 1948, the Federal Government leased the island to the Armdale Yacht Club. Today, the old governor's house forms the nucleus of the clubhouse, while the cells in the former stone prison are used for storage.

A short distance across the water, hidden beneath the forested slopes of deserted Deadman's Island, lie some 400 unmarked graves of French, Spanish and American prisoners, as well as black refugees and Irish immigrants. Some of the hastily dug prisoners' graves appear to once have been marked. A piece of doggerel from Palmer's journal noted "no monumental marble" to indicate the graves, but "the papal cross is plac'd next to the graves where papists rest."

The crosses soon disappeared. Thomas Chandler Haliburton, visiting the prison in the 1820s, noted, "On a small hill to the southwest is the burying ground belonging to the establishment. It is no longer to be distinguished from the surrounding woods, but by the mounds of earth which have been placed over the dead; the whole being covered with a thick shrubbery of trees."

Over the years, visitors reported that shallow graves were being uncovered by heavy storms and human skeletons exposed. Charles Longley built a dancehall on the island in about 1909. He dug up three skulls while gardening there and placed them in the basement of the dancehall to deter thieves from entering it. Someone promptly stole the skulls. As late as 1959, a resident excavating an addition to his house discovered another human skull embedded in the frozen ground close to the shore of Deadman's Cove, located immediately south of Deadman's Island.

In 1998 a developer proposed turning Deadman's Island and
the adjoining area into a condominium complex. Local residents
objected, worried about loss of trees, overall aesthetics and the
site's rich heritage. The Northwest Arm Heritage Association under
its president, Guy MacLean, led the fight. Its members enlisted the
support of various American veterans' groups by informing them
of the long-forgotten graves containing the remains of their countrymen. Ultimately, the Association and its allies succeeded. The
city of Halifax bought the land for $200,000 and declared it a her-
itage site, preventing its commercial development.

Interest and concern continued to grow in the United States for
the unmarked graves of its war dead. At a June 2000 ceremony,
troops from the Tennessee Air National Guard's 164th Civil
Engineering Squadron, then training in Nova Scotia, planted 188
miniature Stars and Stripes on the island, one for each American
buried at the site. They also placed 188 small black flags to sym-
bolize prisoner of war/missing in action, following a practice that
became popular during the Vietnam War.

United States Veterans' groups also petitioned Congressmen and
Senators, and formally asked the American Government to erect a
group monument commemorating the gallant men buried on
Melville Island almost two centuries ago.

They succeeded, and a monument now honours these men who
bravely served their country but ended their days far from home on
this tiny island.

4

THE MAN WHO BURNED WASHINGTON

Crowded in amongst the other tombstones and burial markers of Halifax's Old Burying Ground, almost at its centre, stands a non-descript, weathered, sandstone sarcophagus. Most people might pass it by unnoticed. But anyone who makes the effort to read the inscription engraved on its covering slab, still remarkably legible after almost two centuries, will be rewarded by the discovery of a fascinating chronicle:

HERE
On the 29th of September 1814
Was committed to the earth
THE BODY
OF
MAJOR GENERAL ROBERT ROSS
WHO
After having distinguished himself in all ranks as an officer
IN
Egypt, Italy, Portugal, Spain, France & America
WAS KILLED
At the commencement of an action
Which terminated in the defeat and rout
OF
The troops of the United States

NEAR BALTIMORE

On the 12th of September

1814

- ◊ -

At

ROSSTREVOR

The seat of his family in Ireland

A MONUMENT

More worthy of his memory

Has been erected

BY

The noblemen and gentlemen of his county

AND

The officers of a grateful army

WHICH

Under his conduct

Attacked and dispersed the Americans

AT

Bladensburg

On the 24th of August 1814

AND

The same day VICTORIOUSLY entered

WASHINGTON

THE CAPITAL OF THE UNITED STATES

- ◊ -

IN

ST PAUL'S CATHEDRAL

A MONUMENT

Has also been erected to his memory

BY

HIS COUNTRY

- ◊ -

The military action to which this epitaph refers was one of the most humiliating defeats a nation can suffer. In 1814, the American capital, Washington, was occupied and destroyed by an army led by one of Britain's most able and respected generals. At his moment of triumph, Major General Robert Ross was cut down. His body was brought to Halifax and buried.

Earlier that year, in April, an event across the ocean in Europe changed the course of the War of 1812. Under the Duke of Wellington, British, Portuguese and Spanish forces finally drove the invading French from the Iberian Peninsula, ending the Peninsular War. With the conclusion of Wellington's campaign, more British troops became available to fight in North America. For the first time since President Madison declared war, the British were in a position to undertake major land offensives, instead of their largely defensive actions of the past two years.

The cessation of hostilities in Europe also freed up Royal Navy warships previously employed against the French. To the British, it made sense to capture as much American territory as possible to improve their position during the peace negotiations then taking place. For the previous few months, Rear Admiral Sir George Cockburn had raided the American coastline to great effect. Now he planned to strike farther inland, against Washington and Baltimore.

Many viewed these proposed attacks as retaliation for earlier American raids against Canada, in particular the needless burning of York (now Toronto) and, to a lesser degree, Newark (now Niagara-on-the-Lake) in 1813, which destroyed much public and private property.

Representatives negotiating peace terms in the Belgian city of Ghent warned Americans of British preparations for an attack. Despite the warning, the Americans made few arrangements for the safety of their capital. At the time, Washington was a small town of about 8,000 people that had been carved out of the Potomac swamps a few years earlier. Secretary of War John Armstrong refused to believe the city could become a target of the British. In his opinion, a more likely objective was Baltimore, a wealthy seaport, naval base and homeport for many successful privateers. It was an opinion reinforced by Cockburn's vow to burn every house in the port city.

Finally, word of large-scale British preparations goaded the administration into action and they created a new Military District, comprising Maryland, the District of Columbia and northern Virginia. Unfortunately, Madison overruled Armstrong's selection for the district's commander and chose a leader on the basis of political connections, rather than military competence.

Brigadier General William Winder, a veteran of battles on the Canadian border, was captured at the Battle of Stoney Creek and had been only recently exchanged. He was a nephew of Maryland Governor Levin Winder, whose militia would provide the bulk of the initial forces to meet any British invasion. Winder's shortcomings were many, the most serious being his incompetence and indecision. He was incapable of thinking ahead. He could not delegate, and in the end drove himself to almost total exhaustion.

Brigadier General William Winder owed his appointment as commander of the American defenders of Washington to his political connections.

The regular soldiers immediately available to Winder consisted of about 625 infantrymen, cavalry and marines, as well as the garrisons of a few forts. The more numerous militia were under equipped—many didn't even have weapons—and poorly trained. American Commodore Joshua Barney commanded a small gunboat flotilla for coastal defence, but he and his 400-odd "flotillamen" were trapped up the Patuxent River by Admiral Cockburn and his fleet. Winder asked for 4,000 militia to be called out immediately. Armstrong refused, concerned the militia might not answer the call unless the threat was imminent.

After several months of raids, the British were thoroughly familiar with the Chesapeake Bay area and could move much more quickly by water than American troops could move by land. With more soldiers, the British now had the capability of striking heavy blows against major cities, instead of just modest raids.

Vice Admiral Sir Alexander Cochrane, who replaced Warren as commander of the North American Station at Halifax in March 1814, favoured a much more aggressive policy than that of his predecessor. He directed his naval forces "to destroy and lay waste such towns and districts . . . as you may find assailable."

Major General Robert Ross commanded the army component of the joint campaign. Ross, a 47-year-old Irishman, had served with great distinction under the Duke of Wellington and was one of his best officers. In the summer of 1814, the War Office sent him to North America with orders to "effect a diversion on the coasts of the United States of America in favour of the army employed in the defence of Upper and Lower Canada." Ross had three of Wellington's experienced regiments, the 4th, 44th and 85th, as well as a 50-man detachment of sappers and miners, along with commissariat and medical services.

Part of Ross's force was a 150-man Royal Artillery rocket brigade, equipped with Congreve rockets. The Congreve rocket, only invented a few years earlier, was a yard-long tube filled with powder. It made a lot of noise but caused little damage.

On July 25, after nearly two months at sea, Ross arrived in Bermuda where he was joined by the 21st Regiment and a company of 75 black Colonial Marines, made up of former American slaves. This brought his command to about 3,400 experienced soldiers.

The expedition sailed from Bermuda on August 3, under Cochrane's strategic direction, and met Cockburn's fleet in Chesapeake Bay. As overall commander, Cochrane chose the force's objectives, subject to Ross's approval. The three commanders discussed their options. The admirals were in favour of an immediate overland attack on Washington, but Ross was not so sure. His men had been weakened by nearly three months of inactivity aboard ship and a fever had broken out during the voyage. He had no cavalry for scouting or flank protection, minimal field artillery to support his infantry and no wagons to haul supplies. He didn't even have a horse for himself.

Ross also had to take into account the effect of the area's well-known summer heat and humidity on heavily laden, marching soldiers. And what about Barney and his flotillamen, known to be up the Patuxent River? In the end the admirals won the day: the three commanders decided to land the troops. The army would test American strength while the navy dealt with Barney.

Cochrane, Cockburn and Ross sailed up the Patuxent to the town of Benedict, Maryland, where Ross and his troops landed on August 19. The road to the capital, some 40 miles away, lay open. On the twentieth, Cockburn sailed further upriver to find Barney. Ross, waiting for cooler evening air, advanced six miles before setting up camp for the night, accompanied by Cochrane.

Cochrane had earlier sent a letter to American Secretary of State James Monroe stating he had orders to "effect measures of retaliation against the inhabitants of the United States for the wanton destruction committed by their army in Upper Canada." The citizens of Washington reacted with alarm when this message reached them and began preparing for an attack, but in an entirely undirected fashion. Under Winder, little had yet been accomplished in the way of substantial measures to defend the capital.

Meanwhile, the President called out the city's militia and asked neighbouring states for assistance. When the militia reported for

Washington burns in the background of this portrait
of Rear Admiral Sir George Cockburn.

duty, several men had to be sent home to get weapons. By August 20, over 9,000 men and up to 50 field guns had mustered and were spread out from Baltimore through Annapolis to Washington. The majority assembled at Baltimore, with 5,000 men and 30 field pieces, and at Washington, with 2,500 men and 12 artillery guns. Winder dispatched most of the Washington militia to the village of Woodyard, Maryland, 12 miles away, where they joined 750 regulars with five cannons. Winder established his headquarters there on the night of August 21.

Shortly afterwards, Monroe arrived. He had taken it upon himself to ride out and scout the enemy, escorted by cavalry. Unfortunately, he had forgotten his telescope and remained at such a distance from the British that he overestimated Ross's force at 6,000 men. He passed this error on to the excitable Winder. At Woodyard, a shortage of camp equipment, combined with half-rations, left many militiamen spending a hungry night under the stars.

As Winder moved to Woodyard, Ross and his men continued their advance in the stifling heat of the hottest August in memory. The British were supported by Cockburn, who was moving upriver with his small flotilla. That night, the soldiers camped at Nottingham, and marched towards Upper Marlboro on August 22. Meanwhile, Winder dispersed his troops, leaving himself open to the piecemeal destruction of his forces by spreading them around too thinly. With about 2,000 troops, and Monroe tagging along, he set off towards Nottingham as Ross advanced on Upper Marlboro.

Winder and his cavalry escort, riding ahead of the troops, bumped into Ross's advance guard. The American general immediately galloped back to his column, yelling for them to retreat, and rushed them all the way back to Old Fields. Most of his men did not even see the British. Ross, no doubt somewhat puzzled by the American reaction, continued to Upper Marlboro and set up camp.

Sometime during the night, Ross decided to make a quick dash for the capital—a dash that would take him through the town of Bladensburg. Bladensburg was a crossroads located on a ridge on the east bank of the Eastern Branch of the Potomac River. Main roads from Baltimore, Annapolis and Upper Marlboro met there and formed a single road leading westward across a sturdy 30-yard-long bridge. This road then split into two about 200 yards past the bridge, the road on the left leading to Washington and the other to Georgetown. Above Bladensburg, the river could be forded easily in several places. Below the village it became a deep, quarter-mile-wide stream, almost impassable without bridging.

On August 23, Brigadier General Tobias Stansbury's largely untrained Maryland militia brigade of two regiments occupied Lowndes Hill, a dominating feature overlooking the roads leading into Bladensburg from the east. Lieutenant Colonel Joseph Sterrett's 5th Maryland Infantry Regiment, which Winder placed under Stansbury's command, joined him. By now, Commodore Barney had destroyed his gunboats and was force-marching his men towards Washington's Navy Yard, hoping to avoid being cut off by Ross's advance.

With Barney's gunboats out of the picture, Cockburn also joined Ross, hoping to steel the general's resolve. Cochrane remained at Benedict. Since landing, Ross's force had been increased by several Royal Navy assets: a 700-man Royal Marine battalion, a 150-man Royal Marine Artillery rocket corps, 100 naval gunners and approximately 275 sailors to carry supplies and tow guns and ammunition wagons. Ross now commanded 4,370 men organized into three brigades, supported by one 6-pounder and two 3-pounder guns, plus 60 rocket launchers.

The British army set off on the afternoon of August 23, heading for Bladensburg by way of Old Fields. Each sweating soldier was heavily laden with three days' rations, 60 cartridges, a pack, canteen and weapon. The soldiers were followed by sailors pressed into service like pack animals, also sweating—and swearing. About 20 or so horses had been rounded up, enough to mount the senior officers and a few infantrymen to act as cavalry scouts. That night Ross's men encamped about halfway to Old Fields.

By now, most senior American civil and military officials were becoming alarmed by the British advance, Winder perhaps more so than the others. On the evening of August 22, at Old Fields, a false alarm kept Winder and his troops awake most of the night. Madison and his Cabinet arrived the next morning; the President reviewed the troops and delivered an inspirational address.

Rumours abounded as to the location of the British. With each report, Winder ordered troops to move hither and thither, only to countermand his orders and issue different ones when he received fresh information. His men were being worn out before they even met the British on the field of battle. He told Stansbury to hold Bladensburg as long as possible and retire directly on Washington if forced to retreat. Monroe arrived at Bladensburg late that evening, recommended that Stansbury attack Ross's rear, and then rode off. Neither man had any idea where Ross was.

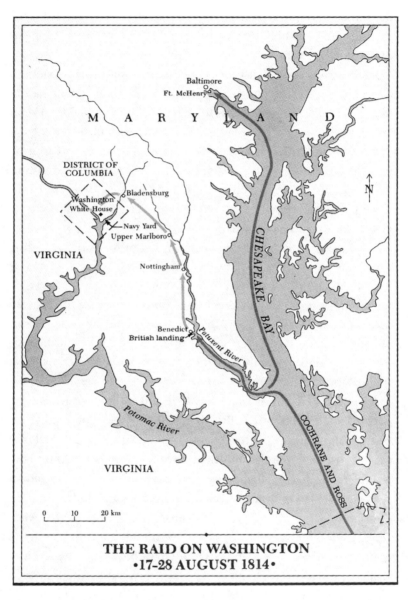

THE RAID ON WASHINGTON
•17-28 AUGUST 1814•

The British raids on Washington and Baltimore in August 1814 took the Americans by surprise and brought the war deep into American territory.

Later, a message arrived from Winder informing Stansbury he was falling back to the capital and confirming that the two bridges across the Eastern Branch below Bladensburg were prepared for destruction. Winder then reiterated his earlier order to Stansbury: hold Bladensburg as long as possible. When Stansbury realized he and his men were the lone American defenders east of the river, he panicked. At 3 am, he hurriedly awakened his troops and rushed them across the river towards Washington. In his haste he forgot to destroy the bridge.

When a dispatch arrived from Winder directing him to reoccupy Bladensburg, Stansbury repositioned his troops, but instead of reoccupying Lowndes Hill, a naturally strong position, he selected an area about two-thirds of a mile west of the bridge, just north of the road to Washington. Monroe joined Stansbury to offer his assistance. Winder soon arrived, with Madison and his Cabinet galloping behind.

Stansbury's position sloped gently down to the river. Thickets lined the west bank, especially south of the bridge. The eastern bank was more open except for a few scattered houses. Between the Georgetown Road and the Washington Pike, a large orchard spread up the slope almost to its exposed crest. Another 150 yards beyond the fork, civilian volunteers hastily erected a strong U-shaped breastwork for heavy guns, only to discover that no one had provided any.

Stansbury commandeered the earthwork for Sterrett's 6-pounders. To cover his flanks, he placed infantry companies north of the Georgetown Road and south of the bridge. He positioned the remainder of the two infantry regiments, along with Sterrett's Maryland riflemen, in the orchard, line abreast but with no fields of fire. By 11 am, his dispositions complete, Stansbury did nothing else to improve his position. Neither his infantry nor artillery could fire on the still-intact bridge or likely fording-places.

About noon, additional troops arrived from Washington under Brigadier General Walter Smith. While Stansbury and Smith argued over seniority, Monroe appeared and began fiddling with the position of the three infantry regiments. He moved them even farther back, out of the orchard to the crest of the hill. As Stansbury and Smith continued to argue, Winder arrived and began checking Stansbury's dispositions. He left Monroe's "adjustments" intact and failed to order the bridge destroyed. His one sensible move was to reposition five guns forward.

Smith's 1,700 reinforcements arrived none too soon. They were a sizeable increase to the American defences. Smith positioned his brigade astride the Washington Pike, about one mile to Stansbury's right rear. There, a hill faced open fields that ended at a steeply banked creek about 400 yards away, crossed by Tournecliffe's Bridge. On a knoll to the south of the road, Colonel Beall's recently arrived Annapolis militia regiment anchored the right flank of the position. On the other side of the road, two lines of infantry stretched northwards, augmented by six more 6-pounders. A large gap remained between Beall and the other side of the road, intended for Barney's guns—if he could get there on time.

In front of the position, a small militia battalion deployed on the western side of the creek bed. To guard against any flanking movement by the British to the north, Smith posted two rifle companies and a cavalry troop along the Georgetown Road, near three field guns. Although Smith's layout was sound, it was not coordinated with the units farther forward and could not effectively support them.

Winder's poor leadership would soon prove disastrous. With all his resources deployed, he did not maintain a reserve to employ at a critical time. He did not even establish a command post to control his troops who, after four days of forced marches and countermarches in the August heat with little sleep and few rations, were tired, dirty, hungry—and confused. This hastily assembled, largely untrained and poorly equipped 5,000–6,000 man force was about to do battle with 4,000 of Wellington's renowned "Invincibles."

Ross set off at 4 am on August 24 and reached Bladensburg at midday. He halted while his advance guard reconnoitred the deserted village. The troops had been marching for about eight hours, the last few in the broiling sun. Dozens had fallen by the wayside, half-delirious from sunstroke or heat prostration in their heavy woollen uniforms. Yet most still proudly marched in step, sweating and choking in the enveloping dust clouds.

While the British advance guard crept through the village, the main column turned right and occupied the reverse slope of Lowndes Hill, out of sight of the Americans. Ross looked across the river. To him it seemed that Winder was strongly posted. The hill-side swarmed with troops and bristled with guns. He began to have doubts. His force was small, and he was far away from the ships. Nevertheless, other officers seemed anxious to attack.

When the advance guard found Bladensburg clear, Ross let the attack begin. Colonel Thornton's light brigade—the 85th, and the light companies of the 4th, 21st and 44th—attacked, although the two other brigades had not yet arrived. The soldiers formed up behind Lowndes Hill, and marched over the hilltop and down into the town, heading straight for the bridge. As they advanced, scattered gunfire flashed along the far bank of the river.

The untrained and inexperienced Americans fired too early, their first volleys merely wasting ammunition. As the British reached the bridge, some shots began to find their targets and a few redcoats crumpled to the ground. Royal Marines fired Congreve rockets, which screamed over the heads of the surprised militiamen. The rockets spewed smoke and flame, but caused little damage other than terrifying the raw troops.

Winder knew the rockets were harmless and tried to steady his men. At the same time, he suggested that President Madison and his Cabinet members, who were seated nearby on their horses, move farther back. Madison, vaguely expecting to somehow preside over the battle as the constitutionally appointed Commander-in-Chief, stared over the battlefield in startled disbelief. Events were already far beyond his power to control or even influence. Remarking that military matters should be left to military men, he rode off to the rear, his disillusioned Cabinet following.

The few American guns closest to the bridge kept up a steady fire on the British, but their crews had been issued with solid shot instead of the more useful grape or canister. Yet they did break up the initial British advance, driving the redcoats behind nearby houses and walls for cover. Some skirmishers in the scrub near the bridge fired a volley and fled, the first of many to leave the field of battle in haste that day. Others quickly followed.

While the British fired their rockets as quickly as they could reload the tubes, Thornton charged the bridge on his grey horse, sword flashing in the sunlight. His men followed at a run. An artillery salvo miraculously missed Thornton but cut down a handful of his soldiers. Before the gunners could reload, more redcoats came pouring across the bridge and fanned out along the river.

The British quickly moved up the slope, working their way into the orchard. They closed rapidly, forcing the militia gunners to withdraw. The militiamen managed to get five guns away, but spiked the sixth. They galloped down the Georgetown Road along with two infantry companies, whose riflemen joined the 5th Maryland on the crest. On the left flank, the British 44th Regiment forded the Eastern Branch at several locations and formed up for an attack.

Winder's first clue that all was not well was the sight of his troops streaming towards him in panic. The orchard blocked his view of the forward positions and he had no idea what was happening. His solution was to counterattack, and he ordered Sterrett forward. Some 600 Marylanders advanced. British fire tore into them from the front and the right, and was soon joined by fire from the left as the 44th moved up the hill. Sterrett halted just behind the abandoned artillery position, having driven elements of the light brigade back to the bridge.

It was hard to say who was more surprised, the ragtag Americans rolling down the hill shoulder to shoulder, or the British sniping from behind cover. The normal tactics of North American warfare were completely reversed.

As the British 85th grouped for an attack, another salvo of rockets crashed into the Americans, causing widespread panic. Frightened militiamen dropped their weapons and ran, most of them impervious to all attempts by their officers to rally them. With the right flank of the forward position now open, the 85th rushed forward and overran the remnants.

Forward, at the Marylanders' new position, Winder ordered the unit to withdraw along with three guns. Then he countermanded his orders, only to change his mind once again and tell them to retreat. When the untrained Marylanders tried to withdraw, they collapsed in disorder, broke and ran. The 44th came streaming up the hill after them. As the American artillerymen and infantrymen ran by, the cavalry, still unused and waiting in a ravine, quickly followed.

Winder escaped and made his way cross-country to Smith at about 2:30 pm. Smith was now heavily involved with the light brigade as it advanced along the Washington Pike, supported by a lone 6-pounder. Barney's guns had finally arrived and set up in the gap, protected by his flotillamen and some marines. The unit at Tournecliffe's Bridge stopped the British momentarily, but was forced back before being outflanked and joined Beall on the right. The British advance continued, only to be halted three times by the determined fire of American guns. Thornton decided to try to outflank the position by swinging to his left, heading for a gap between Barney and Beall.

The British crossed the creek, working their way up from the ravine, when fire from 12-pounders smashed into them, followed shortly by a counterattack from a motley collection of sailors and marines screaming down the hillside. The 85th fell back under the onslaught, and Thornton was badly wounded in the thigh. When Lieutenant Colonel William Wood, the 85th's commanding officer took over, he too went down. Few of the 85th's officers remained unharmed.

When Ross arrived at the scene, he sent his aide back to bring up the 1,460-man 2nd Brigade under Colonel Arthur Brooke, just now entering the village. He ordered Brooke to take the 4th around to the right, while he would personally lead the 44th and remnants of the light brigade around to the left. Calling on his men to follow, Ross galloped ahead, only to have his horse shot out from under him. He quickly mounted another.

By now, Smith's position was in danger of being outflanked on the left, by British troops moving down from the Georgetown Road. As he shifted a regiment to reinforce that flank, an order arrived from Winder to pull back. Smith obeyed instantly and withdrew in good order, much to the chagrin of several of his men, who wanted to stand and fight. Somehow, in the confusion, the order to retreat did not reach Barney. According to him, Beall gave "a fire or two," and then "every man shifted for himself" as the regiment disappeared into the woods, leaving Barney as the lone American defender on the position.

The British flooded up and over the knoll that Beall's men had just deserted, firing down on Barney's position. Barney was wounded and his civilian ammunition-wagon drivers rode off in a panic. Realizing the helplessness of the situation, he ordered the guns spiked and his men to retreat, and then he collapsed. The first British soldier to find him was a corporal, but Barney refused to surrender to anyone but an officer.

The soldier brought back a naval captain, which satisfied Barney's sense of propriety. Displaying the quaint courtesies between enemy commanders that marked the warfare of the age, Ross and Cockburn rushed to Barney and paroled him on the spot. The British took him to a tavern near Bladensburg, where a surgeon dressed his wounds.

Smith continued his retreat towards Washington with about 3,000 men and a few field guns, but was halted twice by Winder with orders to stand and fight. Each time, the indecisive Winder changed his mind and finally told Smith to fall back on the Capitol and form for battle there. Secretary of War Armstrong met Winder at Washington, hoping for the latter to adopt a wild scheme he had concocted to use the federal buildings as redoubts, but panic again gripped Winder and he ordered the retreat to continue beyond Washington. As they passed their homes, hundreds of militiamen left the retreating army to look after their families.

Madison, having retreated to Washington, arranged to meet his Cabinet in Frederick, Maryland, but instead headed into Virginia to find his wife, Dolley, who had already left the Presidential Mansion. The President was still in a state of shock over the encounter at Bladensburg, stunned at the battlefield discipline of the British. His long-held belief—that a free man fighting for his home, no matter how untrained, could stand up to a hired foreigner—had been shattered.

"I could never have believed," he said, "that so great a difference existed between regular troops and a militia force, if I had not witnessed the scenes of this day." His Cabinet scattered in different directions, losing contact with each other and their subordinates. The Government of the United States was in a state of collapse.

The battle was not without cost to the British. Ross had routed an army of 6,000 with about 2,600 men, some two-thirds of his force, claiming he wounded 150 Americans and took 120 prisoners. But his own losses were high: he reported 64 killed and 185 wounded.

The British made fun of the rapidity with which the Americans had fled the battlefield, dubbing it the "Bladensburg Races." Eighteen-year-old Lieutenant George Gleig of the 85th noted, "Never did men with arms make better use of their legs," while Cockburn reported that Ross did not follow up his victory more promptly as "the victors were too weary and the vanquished too swift." Others joked that the only casualty was "an American militiaman who ran himself to death." But in the end, perhaps, the victory was not due so much to British prowess as to American incompetence.

In later years, the Americans tried to salvage what they could from the debacle at Bladensburg, and myths grew up of heroic last-ditch stands and courageous counterattacks. The Americans who fought there knew better. One of Barney's men remarked, "The militia ran like sheep, chased by dogs." Sterrett's official report summed it up nicely: "We were outflanked and defeated in as short a time as such an operation could well be performed."

At 6 pm, after a three-hour halt, the victorious Ross and Cockburn resumed their advance towards the capital. They took only the 3rd Brigade, consisting of the 21st Regiment and the marine battalion. These men had not seen much action and were relatively fresh. The other brigades would follow later. That night Ross led, leaving most of his men at the city's turnpike gate as he, Cockburn and a 300-man advance guard entered the city unopposed. Remembering well how uncontrolled British soldiers had looted captured Spanish towns during Wellington's campaign on the Iberian peninsula, Ross was intent upon taking as few men as possible into the capital.

The British moved down Maryland Avenue, heading directly for the Capitol. Taking their lead from the President and his Cabinet colleagues, about nine-tenths of the city's population had already fled. The British set fire to a number of public buildings, including the Capitol, the Library of Congress and the Treasury. Many of these buildings, including the Capitol, were still under construction. The British generally spared private property, but if there were any resistance from a building or if weapons were found there, they put it to the torch. The inferno's great glow could be seen in the night sky at Baltimore, 40 miles away. The men of 1st and 2nd Brigades, marching down the turnpike, easily recognized each other's faces in the glare.

Ross chose the house of a leading Washington physician, Dr.

The British occupied Washington for 26 hours and burned many of the capital's new public buildings.

James Ewell, for his headquarters. Although Ewell complained to Ross that his home had been looted, he realized the benefit of having the British commander stay there.

Before they could rest, Ross and Cockburn had another task to perform. They started up Pennsylvania Avenue with about 150 men at 10:30 pm. Arriving at the Presidential Mansion, they burst through the front door only to find it deserted. Although the President's wife and the staff had fled, the table remained set for a formal dinner for 40 Cabinet and military officers, apparently in anticipation of a victory. Ross's hungry troops wolfed down the elegant dinner, took a few small souvenirs and then set fire to the residence.

Their work done, the 3rd Brigade camped out on Capitol Hill that night, while the 1st and 2nd Brigades remained at the city's edge, watching the flames. Lieutenant Gleig later recounted, "Except for the burning of San Sebastian's, I do not recollect to have witnessed, at any period of my life, a scene more striking or more sublime." Ross returned to Ewell's house to sleep, assuring him that he and his family were quite safe as, "I am myself a married man, have several sweet children and venerate the sanctities of conjugal and domestic relations."

Early the next morning, a sudden, torrential rainstorm lashed the city, putting out the fires and ending fears they would spread. After dawn, when the storm ended, fresh troops carried on the work of destruction, torching the building housing the Departments of State, War and Navy. The offices of the *National Intelligencer*, a strongly anti-British newspaper heavily critical of Cockburn's depredations along the coast, were next.

In the presence of the admiral himself, British troops smashed the presses and threw type out of the windows. "Make sure that all the Cs are destroyed," Cockburn joked, "so the rascals can't abuse my name any more." When it resumed operation, the newspaper advised its readers that Cockburn had not destroyed the account books, and subscribers were expected to pay their bills.

Ross never ventured into the capital's centre again, alternating between Ewell's house and the army camp. He confided to the doc-

tor that he regretted burning the Capitol Library and would not
have set fire to the Presidential Mansion if the First Lady had
remained, explaining, "I make war neither against letters nor
ladies." He even countermanded his orders to burn the Marine
Barracks when he discovered the fire might destroy neighbouring
homes. Meanwhile, sailors set the city's three rope-making yards
afire, and clouds of dense black smoke soon billowed skywards.

August 25 turned into a sweltering summer day, with not even a
hint of breeze to cool the sweating soldiers, but huge thunderclouds were forming to the northwest. A detachment headed for
Greenleaf's Point, at the junction of the Potomac and its Eastern
Branch, and the site of an ammunition magazine containing 150
barrels of gunpowder. Somehow, as the British were dumping the
barrels down a deep well, there was a massive explosion which
killed as many as 30 soldiers and badly injured another 44. Their
comrades took the injured to a makeshift hospital.

The thunderclouds rolled in on the capital. Lightning flashed, rain
began to fall and a strong wind sprang up. In an instant, a howling
thunderstorm hit the city, the likes of which no resident could
remember. It pulled Lieutenant Gleig from his horse and tossed two
cannons about like toys. Soldiers and citizens ran for cover.

By now, Ross was feeling dangerously overextended. The magazine explosion had unnerved him and the storm dampened his
spirits. Rumours were beginning to circulate of a 12,000-man
American army on the march. He had accomplished much more
than he ever thought possible and resolved to leave that evening.
He issued orders to withdraw after dark, confining the residents by
curfew. The thought of having to leave seriously wounded men
behind, especially those from the arsenal explosion, greatly upset
him. Dr. Ewell assured Ross he would care for the men personally.

To camouflage their departure, the British built huge bonfires at
various locations that evening. While a few soldiers hovered
around the fires, giving the impression that everything was
normal, their comrades fell in and marched off. After a 26-hour
occupation, the British silently left the city. They reached
Bladensburg once again at midnight and paused for an hour's rest.

Ross was obliged to leave 83 more of his wounded there under the care of Commodore Barney, including Colonel Thornton, still recovering from his wounds. The British marched onwards, reaching Benedict on August 29.

Throughout the return journey, no Americans interfered with their movement. In 12 days, the British had marched 60 miles into the enemy's country, defeated his larger army, captured his capital, left his elected leaders scattered and fearful, burned his great public buildings and marched back unmolested. They re-embarked the next day.

At Washington, British troops had been kept generally under control and prevented from looting, tolerated by neither Ross nor Cockburn; they had seven soldiers flogged for various offenses. The same could not be said of the Americans who remained behind. Some Washington residents looted and raided the Presidential Mansion, the Capitol and the Navy Yard. When the Americans returned to the city they found it gutted. More than $1 million worth of public and private buildings had gone up in flames. The government even considered moving the capital farther inland for security and in order to save the cost of rebuilding. It took the American victory at New Orleans in January to convince them to rebuild.

During repairs to the damaged Presidential Mansion, workmen concentrated on its interior, hastily whitewashing fire evidence on the outside and creating the "White" House. Traces of black smudges can still be seen on some of the original sandstone blocks.

The British sailed away on September 6, down Chesapeake Bay to rendezvous with some ships operating on the Potomac. After much debate, the triumvirate of Ross, Cochrane and Cockburn finally decided that Baltimore—a strongly anti-British seaport with a population of more than 45,000 and America's third largest city—would be the next target. The British fleet headed north again, towards their new objective.

After midnight six days later, Ross and 5,000 soldiers with eight horse-drawn guns began landing at North Point at the mouth of the Patapsco River, on the tip of a narrow, jagged peninsula some

14 miles from Baltimore's eastern edge. To make up for losses at Bladensburg and Washington, Cochrane added a 1,000-man naval brigade. The whole force was ashore by 7 am, organizing itself for the march on Baltimore.

A complex of shoals, known only to local pilots, barred the way for Cochrane's heavier ships. Only his smaller and lighter vessels could navigate the 12 miles of channel to Fort McHenry guarding Baltimore's harbour. The Americans already suspected the port city would be the next British objective, and several days earlier 16,000 troops had mustered. Citizens and slaves dug fortifications on the city's exposed eastern flank and the navy blockaded its two approach channels.

Major General Samuel Smith, commanding at Baltimore, anticipated Ross's landing at North Point. He sent his best militia troops there, Brigadier General John Stricker's 3rd "City" Brigade, a 3,200-man force of largely inexperienced Baltimore residents consisting of five infantry regiments, a small cavalry detachment, an artillery company with six 4-pounders and a battalion of riflemen.

Stricker's men camped the night of September 11 about seven miles east of Baltimore. Stricker set up an outpost line two miles to his front, with cavalry another mile ahead of them, based at Gorsuch Farm. At dawn, cavalry scouts reported on Ross's army. Stricker moved his men forward to a position where the peninsula narrowed to a width of about 1,100 yards. He established his defensive line based on Boulden Farm, a small clearing in the middle of Godly Wood on the road from North Point. By 9 am, Stricker was in position. An infantry regiment supported by guns formed the first line. Two more regiments behind them made up the second. The fifth regiment was standing by in reserve. To delay the British, Stricker sent his 150-man rifle battalion, whose rifles outranged British muskets, forward about three miles.

The British moved off in good order, an advance guard leading and flank guards checking the thick woods on either side of the road. Progress was slow as the flank units stumbled around the many tidal bogs. To Stricker's great surprise—he had not heard any

shots fired—his riflemen came rushing back, having heard a
rumour that British troops had landed in their rear. Disgusted,
Stricker sent the riflemen off to reinforce the extreme right flank.

At 11 am, as his advance guard reached Gorsuch Farm, Ross
ordered a halt. The Gorsuch family served Ross and Cockburn
breakfast while the soldiers ate a hasty meal. When Mr. Gorsuch
asked Ross if he would be back for dinner that night, Ross allegedly smiled and replied, "No, I'll eat in Baltimore tonight—or hell."

Stricker decided that Ross's halt presented an excellent opportunity for a quick raid. He hurriedly assembled a 250-man strike
force under Major Richard Heath. As Heath's detachment headed
down the road, it collided with Ross's smaller advance guard, to
the surprise of both.

The veteran 85th rapidly outflanked and forced back Heath's
inexperienced troops. As Ross rode forward to check on the situation, a shot rang out from the woods, passing through his right
arm and lodging in his chest. He fell from his horse. The light companies, hurrying forward to help the advance guard, found him
lying by the roadside, still conscious. He asked them to send for
Colonel Brooke, commanding the 44th Foot and the next senior
army officer.

Brooke, Cockburn and a surgeon rushed to Ross's side. As the
doctor bound his wounds, the fallen general realized the seriousness of his injuries. He took a locket from his tunic, passed it to
Cockburn and said, "Give this to my dear wife, and tell her I com-
mend her to my King and country." Ross was placed on a cart and
taken back down the road towards the fleet. On the way, he lapsed
into a coma, but regained consciousness long enough to call out
"My dear wife" before he died. His aide wrapped his body in the
Union Jack.

Meanwhile, Brooke launched a full-scale attack against the
Americans and succeeded in driving them back. American losses
were heavy: 24 killed, 139 wounded and 50 taken prisoner or
missing. But so were the British casualties: 46 killed and some
300 wounded. Brooke set up camp for the night. Stricker withdrew to Baltimore.

Major General Robert Ross was struck down by a sniper's bullet during the advance on Baltimore.

While the Americans and British fought on land, Cochrane managed to get his warships across the shoals and up the Patapsco River. Unaware of Ross's fate, at dawn on September 13 he opened long-range fire on Fort McHenry, where a huge 30-by-42-foot flag bearing 15 stars and 15 stripes was flying over the ramparts. After six hours of relentless bombardment, Cochrane moved closer for better accuracy. The Americans, battered but not beaten, replied with such intensity that Cochrane was forced to withdraw and recommence his bombardment from long range.

By 10 am, after a wet night, Brooke's forces advanced to find the new, well-defended American position on Baltimore's eastern approaches. Brooke decided to attack after dark, but needed Cochrane's support to stage a diversion west of the city. By the time Cochrane received Brooke's request for assistance, he had already determined the Baltimore escapade should be cancelled and pointed out that he could only provide limited support. He urged Brooke to cancel his planned assault. By midnight, Brooke had resolved to return to the ships.

Due to inadequate communications, Cochrane had no idea what Brooke had decided, but felt he must create a diversion anyway. He sent a handpicked force in small boats to make as much noise as possible with guns and rockets, simulating an attack on the city's vulnerable western extremities. In pouring rain, the Americans detected the presence of the force and opened up with their big guns. The British retaliated with cannon and mortar fire from their warships, illuminating the night with an impressive barrage that lasted until 4 am.

About an hour earlier, Brooke's troops had moved out in much the same way they had at Washington—behind the cover of several blazing campfires burning to simulate an outpost line. At the same time, the battle at Fort McHenry so moved a poetic young American lawyer watching the Congreve "rocket's red glare, the bombs bursting in air" and the Stars and Stripes still flying "by the dawn's early light," he wrote a poem about it. His name was Francis Scott Key and his poem eventually became the American national anthem, the Star-Spangled Banner.

Repulsed on land and sea, the British sailed away aboard *Royal Oak* on September 16, bringing with them Ross's body preserved in 129 gallons of the best Jamaican rum. In Halifax on September 29, his body was landed to the discharge of half-minute guns from 20 warships and received at the King's Wharf by the grenadier company of the 64th Regiment.

Troops lined the crowd-jammed streets along which the funeral party solemnly moved: soldiers slowly marching four deep, arms reversed, followed by the navy's bluejackets; massed bands playing mournful martial music; army commanders and staff officers in colourful full-dress uniforms; the bier, carrying the dead hero's coffin with his sword and plumed hat resting on top; a riderless horse, symbol of a fallen warrior; the firing party; and, lastly, admirals and officers of the fleet.

At the Old Burying Ground, General Ross's coffin was lowered into the grave with full military honours. Soldiers stood to atten-tion with their chins resting on their musket butts, while a clergy-man intoned the sombre words of the funeral service. When it was over, an aide-de-camp moved to the graveside, ceremoniously snapped Ross's sword in half and threw it on the grave. The grenadier firing party of the 64th presented arms, bayonets flashed, and a rattle of musket fire broke the silence.

The procession re-formed and moved out from the cemetery, leaving the gallant and respected officer, a soldier who had forced an American president to flee Washington, alone in the stillness of the sunlit autumn day.

5

FREE, FROZEN AND STARVING

When the British sailed from the Chesapeake after the failed Baltimore attack, they brought with them to Halifax a group of Americans who were only too happy to leave that country: escaped slaves. The slaves, who fled from Chesapeake Bay plantations, came to Nova Scotia with the British for a number of reasons. Some begged the British to take them with them, others were lured with a promise of freedom.

While there can be no doubt about the sincerity of the British to end slavery, to the modern mind many of their actions and comments appear paternalistic and frequently racist. Essentially, the black refugees were dumped in Nova Scotia without any thought for their future. They were given vague promises of acceptance as settlers—without any explanation of what that entailed—by a naval authority, rather than a civil one. No methods were worked out or agreed in advance with the colonial government to receive, control, allocate, settle, feed, clothe, equip, help or care for them.

Even when the flow of refugees started, no consistent, coherent policy was developed, and the authorities generally did little until events forced their hand. The net result was a procedural mishmash, which in the end undoubtedly prolonged the inability of the refugees to become self-sufficient.

What the black immigrants may have thought of their treatment, we do not know. They were largely illiterate, and their opinions are unrecorded. We can only interpret events through the writings of the colonial authorities. Many officials had good intentions, but their actions do not always demonstrate this.

During the Royal Navy's blockade of the Chesapeake Bay area, raids were mounted inland to cut American supply lines and destroy their stockpiles. During these forays, the British realized the potential benefits of bringing thousands of discontented American blacks to their side. Nevertheless, Vice Admiral Warren at Halifax was instructed not to stir up rebellion among the enslaved people. He was told, however, to take aboard his ships any who requested assistance. They were to be welcomed as free men and not as slaves, and sent to various British colonies.

One of Warren's captains, Robert Barrie of *Dragon*, reported, "The slaves continue to come off by every opportunity . . . there is no doubt but the blacks of Virginia and Maryland would cheerfully take up arms and join us against the Americans." Although Warren dutifully passed this information to the Admiralty, they did nothing about it, at least for the time being.

Some of the first former slaves to arrive from the Chesapeake were brought to Nova Scotia in September 1813 when most of the British fleet left the area to winter in Halifax. On October 2, 133 refugees came ashore to begin new lives. Lieutenant-Governor Sherbrooke expressed his concerns to Lord Bathurst about the effect Nova Scotia's harsh winters might have on them, but other black refugees continued to arrive during the winter of 1813–14.

The British fleet returned to the Chesapeake in early 1814 under a new commander. On April 2, the day after assuming command, Vice Admiral Sir Alexander Cochrane gave orders to his raiding parties to distribute and read out a printed proclamation among the American slaves.

Cochrane's proclamation stated he was aware many residents of the United States had expressed a desire to leave the country to enter His Majesty's service or be received as free settlers in a British colony. Any people who wished to do so, together with their families, would be received on board Royal Navy vessels or at British military posts. There, they would have a choice of either joining the navy or army, or being sent as free settlers to British possessions in North America or the West Indies.

They would "meet with all due encouragement," the document stated. In reality, the vast majority of those who chose to accept the admiral's offer met with little encouragement—or any other form of support.

Cochrane went on to instruct his raiding parties to assure the blacks who chose to emigrate from America that they would be given land and not be handed back to their former masters, even when peace returned.

Cochrane's proclamation drew an immediate response from the slave population, and hundreds of black men, women and children from the blockaded eastern seaboard made their way to British ships and freedom. Most came of their own volition, but former slaves whom the British sent back to persuade others to escape were successful too, while British raiding parties forcibly "freed" still others.

The British had a twofold aim in encouraging and accepting runaway slaves: it was a policy that removed a large part of the workforce contributing to the American war effort, either directly or indirectly, and it provided additional recruits for the British armed forces. It also supplied the British with intelligence on the Americans, and created a state of terror among the slave-owners over the possibility of armed blacks in their midst—a deep-rooted and constant fear. Unfortunately, the British appear to have given little thought to the full impact of this policy, which led to long-term problems with the settlement of the refugees.

In the spring of 1814, Cochrane ordered Rear Admiral Sir George Cockburn to try to raise a Corps of Colonial Marines from the refugees and to immediately prepare them for military service. By early May, a considerable number had enlisted, and at the end of the month Cockburn reported to Cochrane, "The new raised Black Corps and Colonial Marines gave a most excellent Specimen of what they are likely to be, their conduct was marked by great spirit and vivacity and perfect obedience."

In combat against the Virginia and Maryland militia, the black refugees proved as sound as the veteran Royal Marines who fought with them. Cockburn noted "their extraordinary steadiness and good conduct when in action with the enemy." Their commander, Major Kinsman wrote, "The conduct of the whole colonial marines during the duties of the day has been marked with the greatest order, attention, and respect to myself, and every other officer of the battalion, and nothing like tumult or insubordination was observed in the demeanor of any individual."

The prospect of armed black invaders, and the possibility they might incite a slave insurrection, certainly alarmed the Americans. The citizens of one Virginia county presented a petition to their governor in August against calling out the militia for any service that would take them elsewhere. At the same time, Virginia's Adjutant General received a report stating, "Our negroes are flocking to the enemy from all quarters, which they convert into troops, vindictive and rapicious [sic] with a minute knowledge of every path. They leave us as spies upon our strength, and they return upon us as guides and soldiers and incendiaries."

The report went on to blame the black marines, knowing the countryside as they did, for the effectiveness of British ambushes, and expressed apprehension over the powerful effect this must have on those slaves who had not yet been able to escape.

The majority of escaped slaves came to Nova Scotia during 1814, with several hundred refugees landing throughout the spring and summer. Sherbrooke reported to Bathurst that he administered them the oath of allegiance and then authorized them "to go to the interior of the province in search of employment," a somewhat vague and unhelpful reaction to their arrival. Almost without exception, the male refugees were labourers or farmers, with a smattering of tradesmen such as shoemakers, sawyers and wheelwrights. With a booming war economy, however, even common labourers could find employment at five to seven-and-a-half shillings a day.

Those who had arrived in 1813 either obtained jobs or received some form of private charity during the winter of 1813–14. The following year, government assistance became necessary. By October 1814, many of the refugees were suffering terribly. The Commissioners of the Poor at Halifax reported to Sherbrooke that the blacks were "in a deplorable state of distress and unable to gain their Subsistence."

Cochrane, in the midst of planning the British assault on New Orleans, advised Sherbrooke "some of the negro families that were lately brought from Virginia are in the greatest misery and destitute of clothing, food and shelter." Cochrane explained that Bathurst had told him orders would be sent to Nova Scotia to provide the refugees with the necessities they required and he understood they would be regarded as settlers in the colony.

Cochrane had issued the proclamation that induced them to come over on the basis of this information. He also wrote Bathurst about the dreadful condition of the black refugees, and hoped Bathurst would direct Sherbrooke "to provide for these poor people until they are settled, when they will become valuable subjects."

Sherbrooke expressed similar concerns, and sent his own missives to Bathurst and Cochrane, detailing the action he took to help improve the condition of the refugees. His letter to the Secretary for War and the Colonies revealed his growing and obvious disenchantment with the whole refugee situation that had suddenly and unexpectedly become his responsibility.

While many of the refugees had undoubtedly been useful when employed as soldiers against the Americans, it was a different story now that they were in Nova Scotia without jobs. Sherbrooke even believed some of them were responsible for their own misfortune: " Though such of them as are industrious can very well maintain themselves as a common labourer here can at this season earn a dollar and a half per day yet the generality of them are so unwilling to work that several of them are absolutely starving owing to their own idleness."

Sherbrooke also mentioned his concerns over the many old and infirm men and large numbers of women and children who could not work. He feared they would become a heavy burden to the government. In his letter to Cochrane, he explained he had already

directed that any who required medical aid or were unable to earn a
comfortable living because of age or infirmity should be received into
the Poor House in Halifax. There, men would receive the same daily
ration allowance as a British soldier, and refugee women and children
would receive the same amount as soldiers' wives and children.

He also pointed out the need for accommodation and clothing, "or the poor wretches would not survive the inclemency of
our winter." Sherbrooke assured Cochrane that everything possible would be done to help the black refugees, while promising
Bathurst it would all be done as reasonably as practicable. He
asked Bathurst about the way in which the aid would be paid, as
he had no funds available to cover such an expense. He also suggested that the Deputy Commissary General in Halifax could
provide any items approved for distribution, but recommended
some sort of coarse clothing be sent from England because of the
high price of such items in Halifax.

The prices of commodities in Nova Scotia had risen during the
war, largely due to the increased size of the naval and military
establishments. Prices for American goods had been high since
1807, as a result of the commercial warfare between Britain and
the United States, which began that year. War increased the
demand for goods and prices rose further. A barrel of flour sold for
40 shillings in 1803, rose to 75 shillings at the start of the embargo in 1807, and then climbed as high as 100 shillings. It never fell
below 85 shillings during the war. By the summer of 1816, the
priced had dropped and it was selling for 45 shillings. Wartime
demand increased the price of local and West Indian goods as well,
but as supply could meet demand, the increase was not great.

In the fall of 1814, an epidemic of smallpox broke out in Halifax
and Dartmouth, hitting the poor particularly hard. Dr. William
Almon was charged by Sherbrooke to report on the disease. He
noted that smallpox was spreading among the black population
and, because of their poverty, the black families were unable to
obtain the necessary care and medicine. He recommended "medical and other comforts be provided for them who are already
infected and that vaccination should be administered to others by

way of prevention and that Mr. Seth Coleman, a competent person, be requested to attend to their relief."

Coleman, a Nantucket Quaker living in Dartmouth, followed up Almon's recommendations and reported in February 1815 that he had completely stopped the spread of smallpox. Altogether, he vaccinated 423 people, of whom 285 were black. As Sherbrooke had promised, the Halifax Poor House looked after several of those unable to support themselves because of sickness or other reasons, at public expense. At the time, an average of 55 persons per day were accommodated there, with about 20 ill enough to be on the sick lists.

Perhaps belatedly realizing the extent of the situation, Sherbrooke addressed the subject of the black refugees in a message he sent to the House of Assembly on February 24, 1815. It was a seminal event in the story of the refugees, as it marked the first time the lieutenant-governor had raised questions of provincial responsibility and land grants. In his message, he noted that the refugees had come to Nova Scotia in the hope of being admitted as free settlers, and "a great proportion of these people, active, healthy, and endured to Labour, have gone to the interior of the Province" where they provided a useful agricultural labour force. He pointed out that the aged, infants and the sick required relief.

Despite the public assistance and private charity extended to the refugees, Sherbrooke believed they should come under provincial care and asked the Assembly to "make provision for the assistance of the distressed among these people, and to facilitate the settlement of the residue upon the forest lands of the Province." It was a giant step forward for Sherbrooke, but a decision would rest with the House of Assembly.

In classic bureaucratic fashion, the Members of the House decided they needed more information on which to base any decisions about the refugees. They asked the Commissioners of the Poor in Halifax to undertake a census, which indicated that at least 705 blacks had settled in the Halifax area by March 1815, including 336 in Halifax itself, 150 in Preston, 72 along the Windsor Road, 49 at South East Passage and Cow Bay and 27 at Porter's Lake. The survey also mentioned the distressed condition of many of the immigrants, as well as the fact that several wanted to work but could not find employment.

At about the same time, Coleman expressed similar concerns on the state of the refugees to Richard Tremaine, Chairman of the Commissioners of the Poor, noting many were becoming needy, and in want of assistance for lack of work. He had been helping them with goods from his store, and felt additional funding was necessary. He also mentioned the many complaints he had received about begging by some refugees, a way of life they had been forced into by circumstances.

Once the Members of the House received the information they had asked for, they replied on April 1, 1815, to Sir John's request for provincial assistance and land grants. Their reply reflected a prejudice not untypical of the time and stated they "observe with concern, and alarm, the frequent arrival in this province of Bodies of Negroes, and Mulattoes, of whom many have already become burdensome to the public." They granted Sherbrooke £500 for temporary relief, but their compassion stopped there. They claimed they were "unwilling by any aid of ours to encourage the bringing of Settlers in this Province, whose character, principles and habits, are not previously ascertained."

They also suggested, "The proportions of Africans already in this country is productive of many inconveniences; and that the introduction of more must tend to the discouragement of white labourers and servants, as well as to the establishment of a separate and marked class of people, unfitted by nature to this climate, or to an association with the rest of His majesty's Colonists" and asked Sherbrooke "to prohibit the bringing any more of these people, into this Colony." Although the slave trade had been abolished in the British Empire, it appeared that many citizens of Nova Scotia were not yet ready to welcome black settlers into their midst.

Sherbrooke bowed to the Members' concerns; perhaps they expressed what he really felt, despite his rhetoric. He said he would attempt to carry out this request and passed their concerns to

Bathurst on April 6. But the House of Assembly's apprehensions had already been overtaken by events.

In his dispatch to Bathurst, Sherbrooke mentioned he had just received a letter from Cochrane in Bermuda. Cochrane was about to send another 1,500–2,000 black refugees, all in need of clothing and provisions, to Halifax. Sherbrooke believed it would be difficult for so many late arrivals to find work. In his opinion, the government would have to pay for their food and clothing, although he felt he would be unable to provide for this large influx in the same way he had for the smaller numbers who had arrived earlier.

Sherbrooke's solution to the question of how to care for the refugees, and how to pay for their care, was one that Bathurst had suggested previously. It called for the placing of all future refugees under the charge of the Collector of Customs. They would be cared for in the same manner as those who had previously been dealt with by the Court of Vice-Admiralty. Under regulations in force since 1808, which were part of the larger British attempt to halt the slave trade, slaves taken from captured American ships had been "condemned as prizes of war or forfeiture" by that court. These regulations ordered the Collector of Customs to "receive, protect and provide" for all black refugees committed to his care by the Court of Vice-Admiralty.

Despite the avowed British aim of ending slavery and freeing blacks, a court that ruled on matters of property and its ownership had been chosen to adjudicate on the disposition of human beings. It was a choice that, perhaps inadvertently, perpetuated the view of blacks as mere chattels. However, once Sherbrooke's method was approved and adopted, the refugees who arrived direct from the United States during the War of 1812 went immediately into the care of the Collector of Customs. The Court of Vice-Admiralty was not involved.

Due to the prevalence of smallpox, Sherbrooke advised Bathurst he would immediately vaccinate all refugees who did not show signs of the disease, and requested compensation for an army doctor whom he ordered to look after them. To encour-

age industrious individuals who were willing to settle and culti-
vate land, he recommended free rations for them and their families on the same basis and for the same duration as the disbanded soldiers and their families who had settled in Nova
Scotia after the American Revolution.

By mid-June 1815, Bathurst approved Sherbrooke's proposal to
set up a depot for the refugees on Melville Island, and he looked
favourably on the questions of land grants. He noted "the advantage which might result from giving to those persons who are
mostly accustomed to agricultural labour, small grants of land by
the cultivation of which they might in a short time be enabled to
provide for their own subsistence and to promote the general prosperity of the province."

Although Bathurst had agreed to Sherbrooke's proposal, in his
reply to Bathurst Sherbrooke expressed some doubt over the
refugees' ability to clear the land. In Sherbrooke's view, on first
arrival the refugees seemed to dread the idea of tilling such barren
and rocky soil as is found in the province. He did hope that once
those who found work in the countryside saw what could be
achieved on the land, they would want to turn to farming.

Sherbrooke promised to encourage any black refugees so
inclined, and he directed the provincial surveyor-general to look
out for and reserve the best available lands where they might settle. But first he had to attend to the more pressing needs of the
latest refugees.

Responsibility for the care of the expected influx of refugees
from Bermuda would now fall to Thomas Jeffery, the Collector of
Customs in Halifax, under the vigilant eye of Sherbrooke. The regulations required the Collector of Customs to keep accurate books
of account for all expenses and to submit them to the lieutenant-
governor for payment by the Treasury. The government paid the
Collector of Customs a guinea as remuneration for each former
slave he received and provided for.

Jeffery took over the now empty buildings of the former prison
on Melville Island to look after the initial processing of the black
refugees, and to provide food, accommodation and a hospital. The

authorities transferred 76 refugees from the Halifax Poor House to Melville Island on April 27, 1815—its first black inhabitants. Due to their poor state of health, several went straight into the hospital. Royal Navy vessels landed almost 700 refugees who had arrived by way of Bermuda during that spring. By May, 600 men, women and children were staying at Melville Island, more than the accommodations were intended to hold. In June, however, the population was nearly halved as refugees were settled elsewhere.

Sherbrooke redirected one of the first groups to arrive at Halifax, some 381, to New Brunswick on May 25, 1815. He thought it expedient to take this action in view of the Nova Scotia Assembly's expressed opposition to any further black immigration. For his part, New Brunswick's Military Commander and Administrator, Major General George Smyth, agreed to take up to 500 refugees, except those unable to earn their subsistence because of age or infirmity. Those were sent to the Melville Island hospital.

From May to August 1815, the Council approved an expenditure of almost £3,100 for Jeffery to look after the refugees, about one-quarter of it for his services. He spent some £2,036 on rations provided by Halifax merchant Lewis DeMolitor. DeMolitor's three-month contract clearly specified the amounts he would be paid—one shilling per day for healthy people and two shillings for those who were sick—and what he would provide.

The steady, if somewhat monotonous, ration for healthy men and boys over age 12 consisted of bread, half a pound of beef or pork, potatoes or peas, Indian meal, molasses, a quart of spruce beer, salt and coffee. Women and girls over 12 years of age received two-thirds of the men's ration, while children under 12 received one-third of a man's ration.

The contract also specified that beef and vegetables were to be made into soup and issued to messes of no fewer than eight adults, each mess was to have a mess pan and every person a spoon. DeMolitor provided cooks and food handlers to prepare the rations and supply the messes in a proper and regular manner. In addition, he paid all expenses associated with preparing and cooking the food, except for fuel, which Jeffery supplied.

DeMolitor also provided medical supplies and employed nurses for the hospital. His other hospital responsibilities included arranging for washing the linen and clothing as well as providing candles and utensils, and covering "every other expense which may be conceived necessary to the comfort of the Sick by the Surgeon who may be employed to attend the Hospital." The surgeon vaccinated more than 500 refugees against smallpox during the summer of 1815.

DeMolitor's contract also specified rations for the sick, detailing the amounts to be received at each meal, depending on whether the individual required full, half, low or spoon diet. The daily allowance for the latter consisted of a pint of tea at breakfast and supper, with half a pound of bread made into panada (boiled to a pulp and flavoured) or pudding, or four ounces of sago, or one ounce of arrowroot for dinner.

Jeffery renewed DeMolitor's contract when it expired in July 1815, but at a reduced rate: nine pence per day for healthy people and one shilling and seven pence for the sick. Once, when Jeffery's deputy, Richard Best, visited Melville Island during his superior's absence, he found that DeMolitor had not provided spruce beer and coffee as per the contract. Sherbrooke subsequently deducted £15 from the contractor's fee.

Between August and October 1815, 141 refugees arrived in Halifax, fewer than the previous quarter. By the end of the year, 900 had come to Nova Scotia. Several moved on from Melville Island, some as far away as Annapolis Royal, and only 59 remained at the depot by year's end. The cost for maintaining them during the second quarter amounted to only £1,405, less than half the cost of the first quarter. The number of people being fed during that period fell from an average of 340 to 254 per day. The number in hospital decreased only slightly, from 39 per day to 35, reflecting the fact that those who remained were probably ill or infirm.

As the winter of 1815–16 approached, Sherbrooke wrote to Bathurst twice in September, pleading for clothing and bedding for the refugees. The supplies promised from Britain earlier had still not arrived. If they did not appear, he felt it would become necessary to arrange for the purchase of warm clothes. This would be a major expense as clothing was considerably more expensive in Nova Scotia than in Britain. The long-awaited shipment finally arrived in October 1815, by way of Bermuda, where Admiral Cochrane had issued some of the items to refugees there. Women's and children's shoes still had to be purchased in Halifax.

In mid-November 1815, well after the dispersal and settlement of the refugees throughout the province had begun, the Lieutenant-Governor reduced the Melville Island staff to three: a surgeon, a clerk and a keeper or steward. DeMolitor received a new contract on December 16 to supply the remaining refugees, as well as any who were forced to return due to loss of employment. The food allowance remained the same, but at a cost of one shilling per daily ration. In January, when Richard Best reported on the sorry state of the refugees' clothing the authorities provided new shoes and warm clothes. During the third quarter, ending in January 1816, 21 refugees came to Melville Island, including eight who had been rejected by the Poor House because they were not transient paupers. Among them were some who had arrived in Nova Scotia before the establishment of the depot and who were now forced to go there during the winter due to sickness or unemployment.

On Melville Island during the next quarter, ending April 1816, the black population remained relatively steady, averaging fewer than 65. By May there were 40 refugees there and another ten in the hospital, the majority suffering from ulcers.

After a year in operation, and with most of the refugees either settled on the land or working, Sherbrooke decided to close the depot. Those in good health were sent to Preston, assigned lots and given provisions.

In June, only eight refugees, who could not work due to age or illness, remained on the island. Sherbrooke placed two of them in the Poor House and sent the others to the military hospital. On June 20, Sherbrooke issued instructions to discharge the depot's remaining employees and provide for the remaining refugees.

Existing records indicate at least 107 black refugees died while at Melville Island. This is borne out by Jeffery, who noted that he received about 800 people, many in a distressed state and afflicted with smallpox and various other diseases. He estimated that not less than one-eighth of this number died. Books of account for the establishment show expenses for coffins. Given the attitude towards smallpox at the time, it is extremely doubtful they would have been buried anywhere else than Deadman's Island, along with French, Spanish and American prisoners of war who died there earlier.

Meanwhile, Nova Scotia's Surveyor General, Charles Morris, who had been directed by Sherbrooke to look for lands on which to settle the black refugees, found a suitable location. He thought they should be settled near each other for mutual support, rather than be spread across the province. On September 6, 1815, he reported to Sir John on available land in Preston, east of Halifax, the site of previous settlements by black Loyalists and Jamaican Maroons. When many of these earlier arrivals departed for Sierra Leone, their property reverted to the Crown. There was enough room for 200 families in a settlement favourable for agriculture.

Some refugees who viewed the land wanted to move at once, to clear the forest and build houses before winter. Morris, who provided his services for free, also noted the advantage Preston offered in being close to the markets of Cole Harbour, Dartmouth and Halifax, which would enable the settlers to sell their produce and any goods they might turn out.

The Surveyor General recommended that compact ten-acre lots be laid out to form a village. The land would be drawn for by lottery; 1,500 acres would be set aside as a commons to supply fuel, fencing and building materials when those on the private lots ran out. He also suggested that no land be granted until the people were actually settled and had provided proof of their determination to make a permanent settlement.

Such a requirement was not a part of land grants given to white settlers; it reflects an unease with the concept of blacks owning the land. Nevertheless, as a result of Morris' report, the government obtained land at Preston, including some owned by whites, who were compensated with equal amounts of land elsewhere.

Regrettably, while Morris had recommended an area of 2,000 acres to settle 200 families, the government only acquired 1,350 acres, resulting in smaller holdings for each family, on land of only marginal quality.

Once the government secured the land at Preston, Morris put forward a plan for its rapid development by the cooperative efforts of 50 of the most expert and active refugees. Morris estimated that sawyers, carpenters and others working together could build two 215-square-foot houses with stone chimneys per day. In six weeks, enough houses could be built for 500 people.

On November 21, 1815, Sherbrooke reported to Bathurst that he had settled 468 refugees at Preston, all in houses, although they were still receiving rations. Unfortunately, in their haste, the men had built the houses of green lumber that warped and split. Most had no floors or cellars. The people, as well as their potatoes, froze.

Another suitable location had been found for the black settlers at Hammonds Plains, west of Halifax, on the route of a proposed new road to Annapolis Royal. Sherbrooke hoped to have the families of some 180 male refugees accommodated there before winter. The men were already clearing land and building houses. Smaller black communities followed on the Cobequid and Shubenacadie Roads, at Beech Hill (now Beechville), Refugee Hill (near the Northwest Arm) and Dartmouth, and on the fringes of Preston and Hammonds Plains.

To help them become established, the settlers were provided with tools, potatoes and seeds for two years, as well as rations. In December 1815, Sherbrooke approved another issue of clothing for the Preston settlers, including coats, waistcoats, pantaloons, shoes, stockings and blankets.

By early 1816, 1,316 black settlers were living in about half a dozen locations near Halifax—838 of them in Preston and vicinity alone, another 293 at Hammonds Plains and smaller groups in the other communities.

In January, a doctor visited some of the families at Preston and reported that several were near death from consumption, probably due to poorly insulated houses, inadequate clothing and a lack of medical attention. The authorities called on Seth Coleman once again, and appointed him to see to the settlers' medical needs from mid-1816 to the end of the year, using the services of qualified doctors from time to time.

In April 1816, Sherbrooke thanked Bathurst for approving his proposals for the refugees, and informed him that seeds and agricultural implements would be distributed to the settlers for the coming season. By now, most lots at Preston had a quarter- to a half-acre cleared, ready for planting. For two years, although food was scarce and expensive due to poor harvests, the government continued to issue rations to the black settlers.

Not all the black refugees settled on Crown land; private landowners anxious to encourage local development also offered them lots. One Council Member offered families 30 acres each at Parrsboro and near Antigonish, plus a cow, providing they cultivated the land for seven years. After that they could dispose of it as they wished.

After the Melville Island depot closed in June 1816, one further small group of blacks arrived from the United States. These were slaves captured on British vessels during the war, whom the American Government decided to free when the British laid no claim to them. On August 23, 36 landed in Halifax from Charleston, South Carolina. These were the last of 1,600 black refugees to arrive in Nova Scotia during and after the War of 1812.

Sherbrooke left Nova Scotia at this time to become Governor-in-Chief of British North America. His replacement, Lord Dalhousie, arrived in October.

George Ramsay, ninth Earl of Dalhousie, a Scottish peer and soldier, had entered the army in 1788 at the age of 18, rising through the officer ranks to lieutenant-general after service in the West Indies, Ireland, Holland, Egypt, Spain and France. He had also been on Wellington's staff in the Peninsular Wars and at Waterloo. On arrival, he immediately took an interest in the refugees. Many were wandering about without any fixed abode and claiming relief daily. On November 15 he asked the Council to develop regulations regarding who was entitled to receive rations, clothing or other assistance.

The Council's recommendations, presented later that month, included taking a census of those entitled to receive aid, storing provisions designated for Preston in Dartmouth to save money, continuing to issue supplies for Hammonds Plains from an agency there, requiring settlers at all other locations to come to Halifax for provisions and denying rations to the homeless and those receiving wages. The Council authorized Jeffery, perhaps the official who best knew the black families, to issue certificates to those entitled to receive rations.

While Dalhousie considered these recommendations, on December 2, 1816, he advised Bathurst that the refugee account was in arrears. This left the settlers in a state of starvation. Their crops had totally failed, and the numbers seeking aid had increased due to those who could no longer find work. Dalhousie believed he would have to continue to provide rations until June 1817, as well as issue any clothing remaining in the stores. Although he also expressed his fears that the refugees would "long be a burden to the Public," he remained hopeful they would eventually become self-supporting.

On December 4, 1816, Dalhousie issued regulations for feeding and clothing the settlers. Only those who had been brought into the province under the proclamation of Admiral Cochrane after April 1815 would be considered refugees. They must be already settled, or almost ready to settle, at Hammonds Plains, Preston or Refugee Hill and must continue living there or on the lands of individual property owners. They must also have previously received rations. "Those who remain idling about the streets of Halifax, instead of settling themselves upon the lands shall not be considered entitled to rations unless by infirmity or other peculiar circumstances they are judged to be objects of charity."

Rations would be issued from depots to be established at Halifax, Nine Mile River and Preston until June 1, 1817, at which time the distribution would cease. The full weekly ration consisted of seven pounds of biscuit, four pounds and ten ounces of pork and two pounds of rice. Men received a full ration, women a half and children a third.

Dalhousie assigned Jeffery to manage the refugees' affairs, assisted by Richard Inglis, a clerk in the Commissariat Department. Any
clothing and blankets currently in stores were to be issued to those
who were most in need of relief.

Later that month, Dalhousie sent Bathurst another report. Its
contradictions reveal his bewilderment. In the report he
expressed the view that the refugees were incapable of hard work
or disinclined to it, but then went on to say that perhaps one-
third of them were industrious and deserved encouragement.
Shortly afterwards, the census of black refugees, submitted on
December 30, 1816, listed 1,619 persons for whom rations
would be required: 924 at Preston, 504 at Hammonds Plains, 76
at Refugee Hill and 115 in Halifax.

In March 1817, Dalhousie received direction to reduce the cost
of maintaining the refugees. He had already planned to do so with
the cessation of rations on June 1. Curiously—or perhaps compas-
sionately—Dalhousie insisted on continuing to provide rations
after this designated cut-off date to those who were limited by age
or infirmity or had been industrious until they could raise their
own crops, as he felt without such support they would starve. He
limited this entitlement of rations to those black families living on
the land, and he reduced the ration to pork and Indian flour alone,
at a cost of five pence instead of ten.

Dalhousie expressed a more favourable opinion of the refugees
in the summer of 1817 after he had visited their settlements. "I
find almost every man had one or more acres cleared and ready for
seed and working with an industry which astonished me."
Accordingly, he provided 1,500 bushels of seed potatoes, cabbage
and turnip seed and fishing nets. He also attempted to find a market for boards and shingles they had manufactured. Then he
ordered the issue of additional clothing during the winter of
1817–18 and the following spring and summer.

But in October 1818, on orders from the Colonial Office,
Dalhousie directed that no more rations were to be issued.
Following this direction, the refugees almost made it through the
winter, until March 9, 1819, when they could no longer support

themselves and made an urgent representation to Dalhousie for help. When the House of Assembly refused to provide any further assistance, Dalhousie authorized a month's rations to see them through to the approaching spring, when he hoped they would find work in the country.

Then, in June, Dalhousie wrote to Bathurst complaining, "These miserable creatures will be for years a burden on Government." It was a startling statement, one based on what Dalhousie believed were the effects of slavery on the refugees' work habits and apparent lack of success. One year later, in June 1820, with the refugees' future still uncertain, he left the province for his new post as Governor-in-Chief of British North America.

While the authorities attempted to help settle the refugees, a proposal recommending they be sent elsewhere was considered. Perhaps mindful of the earlier transfers of black Loyalists and Jamaican Maroons from Nova Scotia to Sierra Leone, various locations were proposed. An opportunity for the refugees to leave the colony for the West Indies, first suggested in 1815, came to fruition under Dalhousie's successor, Sir James Kempt.

On January 6, 1821, 95 adults and children, mostly from Hammonds Plains, sailed to Trinidad, escorted by Richard Inglis. Their favourable reception led others to express an interest in emigrating, but when transport arrangements were later made for those who wanted to go, there were no volunteers. Perhaps the settlers were fearful of being forced back into slavery.

For the majority who remained, it took many years of further provincial assistance before the black communities were able to exist entirely on their own. Enos Collins became one of the committee members who oversaw their relief.

There are many possible reasons for the failure of the black refugees to quickly become established in Nova Scotia; some are social and others the work of nature. According to Dr. Robin Winks, a leading scholar on blacks in Canada, the Chesapeake blacks differed from the earlier black Loyalists: they possessed fewer trained skills, had less education and were more affected by the climate.

So recently had they been slaves that no natural leaders emerged to champion their people. Most were Baptists, which made it hard for them to assimilate into a predominantly Anglican and Wesleyan society. And the timing of their arrival could not have been worse. An influx of white immigrants filled the labour market, coinciding with a general downturn in the economy after the prosperity of the war years.

Those attempting to farm had their crops devoured by an invasion of thousands of rodents in 1815—"The Year of the Mice." "The Year with No Summer" followed in 1816, when frosts in June and July killed crops. An exceptionally severe winter followed. Some whites took advantage of the refugees—Dalhousie claimed they were "opposed, abused and cheated by the old settlers near whom they have been placed." Others exhibited the era's general antipathy towards blacks, which turned into persecution.

Finally, paternalistic attitudes, both public and private, which ensured the survival of many during their first few years in the province, may have in the end contributed to a state of dependence rather than self-sufficiency. However, it was not only black settlers who required government aid. Disbanded soldiers also needed assistance during the same difficult years, and at least one of their settlements disappeared.

One last matter remained to be resolved. Article I of the Treaty of Ghent, which ended the war, was signed on Christmas Eve 1814. It provided for the mutual restoration of "all territory, places and possessions whatsoever, taken by either party from the other during the war." It covered public and private property, including, at American insistence, any slaves. The British and Americans interpreted this phrase differently. Generally the British refused to return any former slaves.

One instance of a British officer turning former slaves over to Americans off the Georgia coast caused a stir in Britain. The *Naval Chronicle* described the incident as a breach of faith. At one time during his term, American Secretary of State Monroe even claimed the British sold refugees as slaves in the West Indies. The British, justifiably incensed, never received a reply to their request for substantiation of these charges, so they declared them "utterly destitute of foundation."

Discussions over the interpretation of the slave question continued until 1818, when both sides submitted the matter to the Russian Czar for arbitration. He did not make his decision until 1822, when he declared the United States was entitled to a just indemnification from Britain for all slaves carried away by the British forces. It took until 1824 for the commissioners representing each side to agree upon a monitary value for "just indemnification": $580 for each slave from Louisiana; $390 for those from Alabama, Georgia and South Carolina; and $280 for a slave from Virginia, Maryland and all other states.

The American Secretary of State at the time, Henry Clay, presented a claim in 1825 for $2,693,120 for the loss of 3,601 slaves. The British rejected this outright, and countered with an offer of $1,200,000 the next year. They finally settled the claim for $1,204,960, equivalent to £250,000, a small price to pay for the freedom of more than 3,000 human beings, although not everyone agreed on what that freedom achieved. One contemporary writer felt the refugees came to Nova Scotia only "to be free, to be frozen, and to starve."

Today, a large part of the province's black population is descended from the Chesapeake refugees. These descendants continue to live in the places where their ancestors originally settled and struggled to survive.

6

SPOILS OF WAR

Neither New Englanders nor Maritimers had wanted the War of 1812. They were fearful of the disruption it would cause to the lucrative seaborne trade in which both regions were involved. As a result, Sherbrooke, as commander of British forces in the Maritimes, established a truce with the New Englanders within weeks of its outbreak.

However, both the Nova Scotia and New Brunswick legislatures took action to prepare for the possibility that violence would break out in the region. In Halifax, authorities repaired the crumbling fortifications of the Citadel, equipped the Prince of Wales Martello tower with cannons and added a bombproof arch to it. They completed a new Martello tower on George's Island. They also established artillery batteries at Liverpool, Yarmouth and Pictou; erected blockhouses at Lunenburg, Parrsboro and Guysborough; constructed ammunition magazines at Chester, Lunenburg, Shelburne, Yarmouth, Digby, Windsor, Parrsboro, Pictou and Guysborough; and built a guardhouse at Annapolis Royal.

Militiamen were called out to provide coastal defence and to act as escorts and guards for prisoners of war held at Melville Island. In June 1813, Sherbrooke reported militia detachments stationed at Shelburne, Yarmouth, Parrsboro and Guysborough, while other militiamen patrolled the coast from the armed sloop *Gleaner*.

New Brunswick was more vulnerable than Nova Scotia to land-based invasion. The Provincial Assembly renewed the militia law that was about to expire just before the war started. They put £10,000—an incredible amount at that time and twice the province's annual revenues—at Sherbrooke's disposal for provincial defence. New fortifications were constructed throughout the colony and old ones, such as Fort Cumberland (the former French Fort Beauséjour), were repaired under the watchful eye of Lieutenant Colonel Joseph Gubbins, a British Army officer who had been appointed inspecting field officer of the New Brunswick militia in 1810. In addition, the Mi'kmaq were promised gifts and supplies to ensure their neutrality.

Generally, public spirits ran high as preparations were made for the expected clash with the Americans, accompanied by energetic activity in the province's militia units. But it was difficult to convince men to join up for one shilling a day, when work constructing military fortifications in Saint John and Halifax paid seven and a half.

There was no support for the war in New England, where it was dubbed "Mr. Madison's War." It was particularly unpopular in Massachusetts under Governor Caleb Strong. A secessionist movement, which proposed to take New England out of the United States and create a northeastern confederacy, had already sprung up before the war. The war itself only added to the New Englanders' disenchantment, both with the central government at Washington, which they saw as trampling on states' rights, and with the Americans from the South and the West whose habits, views and interests they regarded as completely different from their own.

New England's bitterness came to a head in the closing months of the war, at the same time that American and British delegates were negotiating a peace treaty in Ghent, Belgium. In December 1814, Federalist representatives from all six New England states opposed to the war (Maine did not achieve statehood until 1820), met in secret at Hartford, Connecticut. They adopted a strong states' rights position and passed a series of resolutions against conscription and Madison's commercial regulations. Only the signing of the Treaty of Ghent forestalled New England's secession from the Union.

Although neither New Englanders nor Maritimers wanted a war, the truce proclaimed by Sherbrooke at the start of hostilities ended in 1814. A committee of the New Brunswick Legislature declared that some American-occupied islands at the mouth of the St. Croix River—the international boundary—were actually British territory. Well aware of the separatist feelings in New England, the Council and Assembly put forward military and economic arguments at their March 1814 session for adjusting the international boundary originally established in 1783, at the end of the American Revolution.

They pointed out their belief that, when recommending the border, the boundary commission had made a mistake in identifying the headwaters of the St. Croix River. This error gave the United States a large tract of wilderness country, which was clearly included within the ancient limits of the Province of Nova Scotia—before New Brunswick was created in 1784—and upon which very few American citizens had yet settled.

During the Revolutionary War, an American amphibious force had even attacked the British timber base on Penobscot Bay, only to be defeated by a Royal Navy squadron. Yet, at the end of the war, the British gave up the valuable tract of timberland between the Penobscot and the St. Croix.

The New Brunswick Legislature hoped that, at the peace conference that must inevitably follow the war, the British delegates would insist on "an alteration of the western boundary of this province." Both the province's lieutenant-governor, Sir Thomas Saumarez, and the colony's resident agent in London, Edward Lutwyche, urged Lord Bathurst to consider the recapture of the Passamaquoddy islands, which the Americans had occupied secretly in 1791.

They also recommended the Penobscot River as a more natural boundary that would resolve the inconveniences of the present border. It would allow a shorter route from New Brunswick to Lower Canada through the largely uninhabited wilderness of northern Maine, at the same time making the Saint John River less vulnerable to attack.

The existing border galled many New Brunswickers who were mindful of the old French colony of Acadia, which extended to the Penobscot. Indications that many citizens of eastern Maine, at that time a district of Massachusetts, would not vigorously oppose annexation added fuel to the fire. This was all Bathurst needed to hear, and he ordered Sherbrooke to occupy that part of Maine "which at present intercepts the communication between Halifax and Quebec," leaving the details to the lieutenant-governor.

The conquest of eastern Maine appealed to Sherbrooke for several reasons. Its lands bordered on British territory in New Brunswick, its population was small, its defences weak and a large number of its residents were sympathetic to Britain. Sherbrooke was an experienced military officer. Even the Americans whom he conquered commented favourably on his "splendid talents and courtly manners," noting he had "more show and more the air of authority and command" than many other leading men.

In the summer of 1814 Sherbrooke would take all of Maine, from the St. Croix to the Penobscot. The "Castine Expedition" was the only operation of the entire war that had the objective of occupying and holding American territory.

Sherbrooke intended to mount a joint army-naval expedition with Rear Admiral Edward Griffith, using soldiers from the Halifax and Bermuda garrisons. To test the strength of American defences and the reaction of Maine's citizens to a British invasion, a small raid was carried out on June 21, under Captain Robert Barrie of the Royal Navy, against two forts in the towns of Thomaston and St. George, west of Penobscot Bay.

Barrie's men successfully blockaded the river, captured the forts and spiked their guns, in the process seizing four ships loaded with lime and lumber. A Boston newspaper described the incident by scoffing, "They who were for disputing with England the dominion of the ocean cannot defend their own inlets; they who urged war for the avowed purpose of effecting a Free Trade, have now no trade at all; they who were for conquering Canada cannot protect their own territories."

A larger expedition against Moose Island in Passamaquoddy Bay followed under Captain Sir Thomas Hardy, in whose arms Britain's greatest admiral, Horatio Nelson, had died at Trafalgar in 1805. Hardy's squadron, including *Ramilles* (74 guns), several small brigs and two troop transports carrying the 102nd Regiment, rendezvoused at Shelburne on July 7 with Lieutenant Colonel Andrew Pilkington. Pilkington was an able officer who knew the local situation well from his several years as Deputy Adjutant General at Halifax and who had sailed from that city two days earlier.

He was accompanied by Lieutenant Colonel Gustavus Nicolls of the Royal Engineers, an officer familiar with Moose Island, and a detachment of Royal Artillery. Nicolls's orders stated that he was to put the island into "a respectable state of defence as soon as it is in our possession" by constructing "such fieldworks or other defences as he may think necessary for its security." Hardy's orders were much more direct: he was to occupy and maintain possession of the islands in the Bay of Passamaquoddy.

Since the operation was a preliminary one, Sherbrooke decided not to command it personally. Both Hardy and Pilkington felt surprise was essential for the success of their mission. They had chosen Shelburne rather than Saint John as the location for their rendezvous, to avoid alerting the Americans to their purpose. The plan worked, and Hardy caught the Americans off-guard.

At mid-afternoon on July 11, Hardy's fleet dropped anchor off Moose Island near Eastport. Although the citizens of Eastport had declared in 1812 that they had no desire for hostilities between the two nations, a few regular soldiers of the United States Army had occupied both Eastport and nearby Fort Sullivan. The presence of these soldiers had alarmed New Brunswickers, who saw it as a possible prelude to a full-scale invasion of the province, especially when the American garrison later seized a British merchant ship.

Hardy and Pilkington sent Lieutenant Oates, Sherbrooke's aide who was accompanying the expedition, ashore in a boat under a flag of truce. He was bearing a joint summons to the American commander, Major Perley Putnam of the 40th Infantry Regiment, to surrender. The summons advised him that due to the weakness of the fort and garrison under his command and his inability to defend Moose Island, resistance would only result in the unnecessary spilling of blood.

Putnam was given five minutes to decide upon an answer. "In the event of your not agreeing to capitulate on liberal terms," the summons added, "We shall deeply lament being compelled to resort to those *coercive measures* which may cause destruction to the town of Eastport, but which will ultimately insure us possession of the island."

Putnam initially rejected the demand, probably for the sake of appearances, but when British soldiers began to board their landing boats, he quickly ordered the American colours hauled down before the troops reached the shore. When they landed, he handed them his letter of surrender, noting, "This I have done to stop the effusion of blood, and in consideration of your superior force."

He turned Fort Sullivan and its stores over to the British and he and his 86-man garrison became prisoners of war, although the officers were permitted to go to the United States on parole. Among the captured ordnance and other stores were 12 guns of various sizes, 100 muskets, gunpowder and several cartridges and cannon shot, as well as six swords with belts and scabbards and one United States ensign.

Hardy and Pilkington issued a proclamation on July 14 in the name of the Prince Regent. It stated that all American municipal regulations would remain in force, but required that everyone on the island appear at the Eastport schoolhouse to declare their intention to take an oath of allegiance to King George III or leave the island within seven days. Two-thirds of the population of 1,500 agreed to become British subjects. Moose Island (including Eastport) and the adjacent Allen's and Frederick's Islands were annexed to New Brunswick, with Lieutenant Colonel Gubbins as military governor.

Nicolls oversaw the construction of defensive batteries around Eastport, and Fort Sullivan was renamed Fort Sherbrooke. The customs house reopened and trade recommenced. In accordance with the "Articles of Capitulation for the Surrender of Moose Island," the British occupation was benign and conformed to Article 3: "Every respect will be paid to private property found on Moose Island belonging to the inhabitants thereof."

When Hardy and Pilkington left Eastport on July 24, some of the town's prominent citizens presented them with an address that gratefully acknowledged the liberal and honourable conduct observed by the British towards them and their property. They added that "the order and discipline of the Navy and Army, and the care to prevent injury by them has ensured us protection and freedom from insult in what we hold most dear, our families and domestic firesides."

A strong detachment of the 102nd Regiment remained to garrison the island. When they finally withdrew in 1818, four years after the war ended, they would become the last British troops to leave the United States.

The ease with which the British occupied Eastport and the willingness of American citizens to change their allegiance caused great apprehension along the New England coast. All the communities, including cities such as Portland and Boston, wondered if they would be attacked next. In many places, business came to a halt as the residents prepared to move themselves and their possessions to safer locations. Unknown to them, Sherbrooke intended to advance only as far as Penobscot Bay, where he planned to re-establish the old border along the line of the Penobscot River. Towns beyond the old border had no reason to fear the British.

In Halifax, Sherbrooke had been preparing for the next phase of his plan, while he awaited the arrival of additional troops from Gibraltar. When they arrived under Major General Gerard Gosselin, Sherbrooke left two regiments in Halifax for defence, and for the next invasion chose the 29th, 62nd and 98th Regiments, along with two companies of the 7th Battalion, 60th Regiment and a company of the Royal Artillery—comprising some 2,500 veteran troops in total.

The force sailed from Halifax on August 26 in ten transports escorted by the warships *Dragon* (74 guns) and *Endymion* (50 guns), the frigate *Bacchante* (38 guns) and the brig-sloop *Sylph*

(8 guns). Their commander was Rear Admiral Edward Griffith, a talented, affable, well-mannered and mild-tempered man, somewhat younger than Sherbrooke. They were bound for the town of Machias on the rocky coast of Maine, about halfway between Passamaquoddy Bay and the mouth of the Penobscot.

Very early on the morning of August 31, the invasion force came across the British ships *Bulwark* (74 guns), the frigate *Tenedos* (38 guns), the 18-gun brig-sloops *Rifleman* and *Peruvian*, and the armed schooner *Pictou*, enforcing the blockade against the American coast. Captain Pearce, commanding *Rifleman*, informed Griffith that an American frigate, *Adams* (28 guns), leaking badly from running hard aground on a shoal off the Maine coast on August 17, had taken refuge at Hampden, some 25 miles up the Penobscot River, to make repairs.

On learning this, Sherbrooke immediately decided to proceed directly to Penobscot Bay. The chance of capturing an American warship, especially one that had been successfully preying on British shipping in the Atlantic and had captured ten merchantmen, was too good to miss. The attack on Machias could wait. *Rifleman* and the other vessels joined Griffith's squadron, increasing it to nine warships.

On the morning of September 1, the fleet anchored off the town of Castine, situated on a stubby peninsula on the eastern side of the mouth of the Penobscot. At that site, a small garrison of some 28 regulars from the 40th Infantry under Lieutenant Andrew Lewis, reinforced by 98 militiamen from nearby Bucksport under Lieutenant Henry Little, was responsible for defending the entrance to the river.

Although the defences at Castine were well-sited, they had fallen into disrepair since the Revolutionary War, and parts of them were no longer in use. The defenders, equipped with only four 24-pounder cannons and two 3-pounder brass field pieces, sheltered in a small redoubt and a half-moon battery facing the bay.

Sherbrooke demanded Lewis's surrender, but he refused and opened fire with his guns on Lieutenant Colonel Nicolls, reconnoitring the position in *Pictou*. Sherbrooke prepared to disembark his troops, but before he could do so, the few defenders hurriedly spiked their big guns, blew up the magazine and fled up river, taking the little field pieces with them.

Not realizing the garrison was now deserted, Sherbrooke ordered Lieutenant Colonel William Douglas to take ashore his 98th Regiment plus the two companies of the 60th and a detachment of Royal Artillery. Douglas landed in the rear of the town to secure the isthmus and take possession of the heights that commanded the settlement. Castine was captured as quickly, and as bloodlessly, as Eastport had been. The British occupied the fort and took over the courthouse and other public buildings, as well as a few private homes, to be used as accommodation for their soldiers.

Before proceeding upriver, Sherbrooke dispatched Major General Gosselin with 600 men of the 29th Regiment in the *Bacchante* and *Rifleman*. They sailed across Penobscot Bay to its western shore to capture the little town of Belfast, on the high road from Bangor to Boston. They encountered no opposition. With Belfast secure, the main land route by which any relief force from Massachusetts would arrive was blocked, and the Americans were prevented from interfering with British operations farther upriver.

Sherbrooke sent a combined naval and army force, commanded by Captain Robert Barrie of *Dragon* and Lieutenant Colonel Henry John of the 60th, up the Penobscot with the tide at 6 pm on September 1. They reached Marsh Bay near Bucksport before setting up camp late that night. The Americans did not think much of Barrie, who was about 40 years old. They thought him a rough, snappish, self-important man in whom "was nothing gentlemanly, nothing generous, nothing great," and noted that he was "unmercifully rough both to prisoners and to his own men." His naval component consisted of the brig-sloops *Peruvian* and *Sylph*, *Dragon*'s tender, the troop transport *Harmony* and several small armed boats used to disembark the soldiers and cover their landing.

John was younger than Barrie, and the Americans felt John had less bluster and more ability than the naval officer, although they noted he "could without remorse hear of undeserved severity, and witness unprovoked plundering and pillage." His military element of 600 men included the flank companies from the 29th, 62nd and 98th Regiments, a rifle company from the 60th and a detachment of Royal Artillery with two light field pieces.

When the force set off again the next morning, their progress was slowed by heavy fog and a lack of knowledge of the Penobscot's currents and depths. At about 2 pm near Frankfort, which lies on the Belfast-Bangor road, they learned that Captain Charles Morris had run *Adams* aground near the town wharf at Hampden to make his repairs. Morris had been First Lieutenant on *Constitution* during her victory over *Guerrière*, and had been rewarded with instant promotion to Captain.

As the British advanced above Frankfort, where they left *Dragon*'s tender, they noticed Lieutenant Little's militiamen on the eastern shore moving towards Hampden. John dispatched some soldiers to intercept them and, after a brief skirmish, one American lay dead and two more were wounded. Without loss, the British had prevented the Americans from reinforcing their comrades upriver. The British force continued towards Hampden, and disembarked its soldiers at Bald Head Cove, some three miles from their objective, at about 5 pm. A brief encounter followed with some American pickets stationed on the shore, who were easily overcome by grenadiers of the 62nd and a rifle company of the 60th. By 10 pm, all the British troops had landed, including 80 Royal Marines that Barrie had attached to John's force. They bivouacked for the night in pouring rain.

Captain Morris, a resourceful and resolute commander, was preparing to resist the British advance and defend his frigate. Earlier, he had notified Brigadier General John "Black Jack" Blake, a veteran of the Revolutionary War and commander of the local militia, of the British arrival at Castine and had asked him to call out his troops. In response, Blake ordered out units of his 1st Brigade of the 10th Division, Massachusetts Militia, and then rode from his home in Brewer, across from Bangor, to join Morris at Hampden. Morris and his 268 sailors, helped by townspeople and teams of oxen, had already placed the bulk of *Adams*'s 24 18-pounders in batteries. Nine were located on a 100-foot-high hill commanding the river about 300 yards downstream from the wharf where *Adams* was grounded, 13 were on the wharf itself, aimed downriver, and one was in the gap between the two batteries. But Blake's arrival only served to confuse matters and slow down preparations.

Blake and Morris, each with their own ideas on how to conduct the defence, argued over how to proceed. Their discussions were not helped by the reluctance of the townspeople—who were more interested in preserving private property than in organized resistance—to become involved. The civilians viewed such action against experienced troops as madness.

Morris put little stock in Blake's ill-equipped and untrained militia, and was not prepared to risk the loss of his ship by relying on it. So, instead of digging entrenchments or constructing breastworks, the 600 militiamen from the 1st Brigade's 3rd and 4th Regiments and Bangor's 8th Artillery who straggled into Hampden by the evening of September 2 stood idly by without orders, while the two commanders, their officers and even the town's selectmen continued their interminable discussions. Morris had little confidence that he would receive any effective assistance, so he gave directions "to have arrangements privately made during the night for destroying the ship, in case of being obliged to abandon her."

Without sufficient arms or equipment, the militiamen's main efforts were directed toward trying to keep warm and dry, an impossible task in the chilling rain. As the long night wore on and the rain intensified, their enthusiasm for a fight weakened considerably.

Dawn on September 3 saw the entire Penobscot River valley shrouded in a dense fog. The British recommenced their advance at 5 am, but John noted that the fog, which reduced visibility to a few feet, made it "impossible to form a correct idea of the features of the country, or to reconnoitre the enemy, whose numbers were reported to be 1400." His veteran troops moved in extended order: a rifle company as the advance guard, Royal Marines on the flanks and a light company bringing up the rear. Barrie had reinforced John's artillery with the addition of a naval 6-pounder, a 6½-inch howitzer and Congreve rockets. As the soldiers moved along the road on the western side of the valley, Barrie's sailors advanced up the river on John's right.

Although Blake's men had spent a miserable night and were increasingly reluctant to stand and fight, he somehow managed to form them into line of battle. Their line ran along the crest of Academy Hill in front of Hampden, which sloped down to Pitcher's Brook and a small bridge. Many were now equipped with muskets and powder from *Adams*. He centred his troops to cover the Belfast-Bangor road, the only British avenue of approach.

Blake's left flank, under Major Joshua Chamberlain of Brewer, was anchored on the river. His right, under Lieutenant Colonel Andrew Grant of Hampden, was close to a church where it was covered by the last of Morris's guns: an 18-pounder carronade, plus two light 4-pounder brass field pieces from the Bangor Artillery. Lewis commanded this small, three-gun battery, served by the men who had escaped with him from Castine.

Despite their inexperience, the Americans had chosen an excellent position, one that offered them every advantage, although it was without breastworks or entrenchments. Now it was simply a matter of waiting for the British to arrive.

Although he had pressed a local guide, Tobias Oakman, into service, John moved so cautiously in the all-enveloping fog that it took more than two hours to cover the three miles to Hampden, although the fog began to lift somewhat after they arrived. Then, between 7 and 8 am, his forward skirmishers became so sharply engaged with the Americans that he sent half the light company of the 29th Regiment to support them. John's later dispatch to Sherbrooke described what happened next:

> The column had not advanced much further before I discovered the enemy drawn out in line, occupying a very strong and advantageous position in front of the town of Hampden . . . . As soon as he perceived our column approaching he opened a very heavy and continued fire of grape and musquetry upon us—we however soon crossed

the bridge, deployed and charged up the hill to get possession of his guns, one of which we found had already fallen into the hands of Captain Ward's riflemen in advance. The enemy's fire now began to slacken and we pushed on rapidly and succeeded in driving him at all points from his position . . . .

Lewis immediately opened fire with his 18-pounder, but the untried and untested militiamen aimed wildly into the fog. Most of their shots went high and caused few casualties, one of them John's guide, Oakman. The Congreve rockets threw the enemy into confusion, as they had at Bladensburg. This, coupled with a bayonet charge by John's troops, caused the American centre (followed closely by troops on the flanks) to break and flee despite the best efforts of their officers to rally them.

With the rout of the militia, Morris's rear and flank were exposed. When Barrie's flotilla hove into view Morris opened fire, but he was in a hopeless position. He had no choice but to spike his guns and set fire to *Adams* and a nearby storehouse to prevent them from falling into British hands. His sailors quickly followed the example of the militiamen, and escaped in small groups. After a gruelling journey on foot, they reported to Commodore Hull at the Navy Yard at Portsmouth, New Hampshire. Morris was later acquitted at a court martial over the loss of *Adams*, and went on to a long and distinguished career.

The entire battle was over in less than an hour. The British claimed a cost of one killed, one missing and eight wounded, including one officer. Hampden's Old Burying Ground today has the graves of two British soldiers, so it is probably safe to assume that the missing soldier later turned out to be dead. John initially reported American losses as 30–40 killed, wounded and missing, but the actual number was much smaller: three killed and eight wounded. Eighty prisoners, 20 guns and ancillary equipment, as well as 40 barrels of powder, were also captured. According to Barrie, "The enemy was too nimble for us and most of them escaped into the woods."

With Hampden in their possession and *Adams* destroyed, John and Barrie quickly decided to continue their joint land and water advance towards Bangor, leaving 200 soldiers to secure the village. According to American sources, these soldiers promptly took the opportunity to pillage and destroy private property and to jail about 70 of the town's prominent citizens on board an American privateer, *Decatur*. All were released on parole within two days.

While the men of the village may not have stood up against the British, some of the elderly and the women did. One old resident, while holding a light for a British officer, allowed whale oil to drip all over the back of the officer's fine red jacket under the guise of infirmity of age.

Harding Snow, a veteran of the Revolutionary War, refused to kill his cow when a British officer demanded it for meat. The officer exclaimed, "I guess you don't know who you are talking to. You never have seen a British officer before." Undaunted, Snow replied, "I have and I have seen 'em run." "Where did you see them run?" the officer demanded. "At Bunker Hill," the old soldier retorted. The reply so enraged the officer he brought his sword down on a log with such force he broke it.

A more well-known story is that of Mrs. Kinsley, wife of Judge Martin Kinsley. The British took the judge prisoner, burning his sloop in the bargain. Then, as explained by the Hampden Historical Society:

> When some officers spied Martin Kinsley's gracious home, and needing a house for their headquarters during their stay in Hampden, they appeared at the Kinsley home. Mrs. Kinsley's housework had been delayed that morning, what with the battle taking place only yards from her home. So when the British arrived, she was in the bedroom chambers supervising the hired girls. Hearing knocks at the door, she hurried downstairs and saw the officers in their immaculate uniforms. She promptly shut the door and went back to her work. The enraged officers

continued to knock on the door and shouted orders to open the door. Mrs. Kinsley eventually had enough of their rudeness, opened a window in the bedchamber, leaned out and quietly asked them to leave the premises. The officers continued and Mrs. Kinsley finally having her fill of the British, who might be officers but not gentlemen, ordered the hired girls to open the windows, and taking accurate aim, dumped the contents of the chamber pots on their heads. The stunned officers, their uniforms dripping, immediately left the property. Needless to say, neither Mrs. Kinsley nor the premises were bothered again during the British stay in Hampden. Before leaving, one officer was heard to remark if the militia had Mrs. Kinsley in command, Hampden would have been celebrating a victory instead of a defeat.

At Bangor, a truce delegation met the British outside the town to negotiate the terms of capitulation, but the victors would countenance nothing less than unconditional surrender. After a short discussion, the Americans agreed, and the British marched into Bangor with flags flying and drums beating. The British appropriated additional military stores in the town and also obtained fresh food and drink from the townspeople. Alcohol led to several instances of drunkenness and reprehensible looting of private homes by Barrie's sailors. Then they bedded down for the night in the local courthouse along with John's soldiers.

The next day Brigadier General Blake and nearly 200 of his militiamen formally surrendered. They were immediately paroled on promising not to take up arms against Britain for the rest of the war. The British burned 14 vessels and required the town's selectmen to put up a bond of $30,000 for the guaranteed delivery of four unfinished ships to Castine.

In Bangor, when a deputation of Hampden citizens complained to Barrie about wanton destruction of private property, he allegedly replied, "My business is to burn, sink and destroy. Your town is taken by storm, and by the rules of war we ought to lay your village in ashes and put its inhabitants to the sword. But I will spare your lives, though I mean to burn your houses."

In order to win the hearts and minds of the people, however, Sherbrooke subsequently issued orders forbidding such treatment. There was to be no burning except where absolutely required, and the "better class" of people might be allowed to keep their arms for personal protection, provided they did not use them against the British.

After a 31-hour occupation, John and Barrie left Bangor, taking six vessels with them as prizes. At Hampden, they burned the 16-gun privateer *Decatur* and two merchant ships, confiscated personal arms and powder and destroyed the town meetinghouse. As Morris's cannons on the hill were too heavy to carry away, British soldiers broke off their trunnions to render them useless, but they loaded the guns on the wharf onto their boats. Additionally, the British imposed a bond of $12,000 on the town for unfinished vessels to be delivered to Castine. By September 9, the small force had rejoined Sherbrooke. It was one of the earliest examples of army and navy cooperation in a successful amphibious operation.

Behind them, the resentful citizens of Hampden and Bangor vented their anger not so much upon the British as upon Brigadier General Blake. His effigy was shot, hanged and burned. His poor showing at Hampden equated with treason in the minds of many, and he was in fear of his life. A court of inquiry conducted in 1815 acquitted him of all charges, a decision based on the inferior forces at his disposal.

A year later, a court martial of Lieutenant Colonel Grant and Major Chamberlain (grandfather of Joshua Chamberlain, hero of the Little Round Top at the Battle of Gettysburg during the Civil War), who had commanded the left and right flanks respectively at Hampden, found Grant guilty and suspended him from command for two years. Chamberlain was acquitted.

Once Sherbrooke learned of John and Barrie's success upriver, he directed Major General Gosselin to leave Belfast and return to Castine on September 6. With the line of the Penobscot now secure, Sherbrooke next moved against Machias, about 78 miles to the east, the original objective of his expedition. On September 9 he sent Lieutenant Colonel Pilkington and the 29th Regiment, with detachments from the 60th Regiment and Royal Artillery, to occupy the town. They were carried in ships commanded by Captain Hyde Parker of *Tenedos*, who had captured Benjamin Babcock and his comrades a few months earlier. The next evening, they landed at Bucks Harbour, some 10 miles south of Machias.

Despite the ever-present danger of ambush along the small trail leading through difficult country to Machias, Pilkington considered the advantage of a night march to outweigh the risk. By daybreak, "after a most tedious and harassing march," the exhausted column reached Fort O'Brien and its battery on the coast about five miles south of Machias. The fort was commanded by Captain Leonard with a force estimated by Pilkington to be some 70 regulars of the 40th Regiment and 30 militiamen.

The British approached the fort and battery from the rear, rendering the American seaward-pointing guns, including four 18-pounders and three 24-pounders, useless. A few American pickets were driven in, but the British reached the fort only to find its defenders had fled minutes earlier, leaving everything inside undamaged. "The retreat was so rapid," Pilkington reported later, "that I was not enabled to take many prisoners."

The British subsequently occupied Machias without any resistance, capturing an additional four 24-pounders. Just as Pilkington was about to advance inland, he received a letter on September 13 from Brigadier General John Brewer, commanding the 2nd Brigade, 10th Division, Massachusetts Militia, stating that the militia of Washington County "will not directly or indirectly bear arms, or in any way serve against" the British. When a similar offer was made by the civil officers and principal citizens of the county, Pilkington reported the area secure. At a cost of two men's lives, all of eastern Maine between the Passamaquoddy and the Penobscot was now in British hands.

At Castine, Sherbrooke and Griffith made arrangements for the administration of the captured territory, which stretched for about

100 miles along the coast and several miles inland. With it came about 26,000 new subjects. A joint proclamation assured them of Britain's protection and that payment would be made for all provisions used by the British forces. It also allowed civil authorities to retain the same powers for administering the law that they had prior to the occupation. Sherbrooke and Griffith left Castine on September 18.

In Halifax three days later, Sherbrooke issued a formal proclamation of a provisional government for "all the eastern side of the Penobscot River and all the country lying between the same river and the boundary line of the Province of New Brunswick."

Two ships and about half the British soldiers who sailed to Castine remained there, with smaller garrisons at Moose Island

Lieutenant General Sir John Coape Sherbrooke was lieutenant-governor of Nova Scotia throughout the War of 1812.

and Robbinston, opposite St. Andrews. Sherbrooke appointed General Gosselin as civil and military governor of the area, assisted by Rear Admiral David Milne of *Bulwark*. Gosselin had the soldiers rebuild the old fort and half-moon redoubt at Castine. He added other defensive works, including a new canal through the isthmus, making Castine an island. He also directed all American males over 16 years of age to swear an oath of allegiance or neutrality towards their new masters. Virtually all complied.

Gosselin, regarded by the Americans as a "gentleman with pleasant manners," became a popular figure in Castine during the occupation. He kept his men in order and fostered good relations between the British and the Americans. Many Americans readily accepted the change in their political masters. A company of actors was even brought from Halifax for the entertainment of soldiers and civilians alike. The British set up a customs house and the Americans got on with the business of their daily lives. A large part of that business was trade, and the British started collecting duties on all imports and exports passing through their new port of entry.

During the remainder of the war, American forces never attempted to reclaim the occupied part of the state. Although a seaborne counterattack was discussed in the Massachusetts Legislature and rumours of one often circulated, nothing ever came of it. The British remained in occupation for eight months until April 25, 1815. Then, outmanoeuvred diplomatically by their American counterparts, they agreed to return the territory to the United States by the Treaty of Ghent, signed on Christmas Eve 1814. New Brunswick's brief expansion westward, to the old boundaries of Acadia, was over.

By the time the British withdrew to Halifax in April they had collected almost £11,000 in customs duties. This money was turned over to the Nova Scotia Treasury as the "Castine Fund," with directions from Britain to use it for general improvements in the colony. Sherbrooke, the man whose military expedition made the fund possible, did not get an opportunity to spend it. That task fell to his successor, Dalhousie.

In 1817, Dalhousie reviewed suggestions for the fund's use. He was unhappy with the only college in the colony, King's at Windsor, which accepted only those who subscribed to the 39 Articles of the Established Church, the Church of England. It excluded members of all other religions. He resolved to establish a liberal, nondenominational college based on the university with which he was most familiar, Edinburgh. The bulk of the fund, almost £10,000, was used for this purpose.

On May 22, 1820, in one of his last official acts before departing for Quebec to become Governor-in-Chief of British North America, the Earl laid the corner stone for Dalhousie College on the Grand Parade, on the present site of Halifax's City Hall. Sixty-six years later, Dalhousie moved to its present location in a land swap with the city, so that the citizens of Halifax could have their City Hall in the location they deemed most fitting for its status, the Grand Parade.

As the Castine Fund was created by military action, Dalhousie reasoned that the military should not be forgotten. Given his appreciation of the value of knowledge, in late 1817 Dalhousie

Dalhousie College, Halifax, was paid for with monies from the Castine Fund. It was perhaps the most lasting effect of the War of 1812 upon Nova Scotia.

suggested "the great comfort and advantages that might result from the establishment of a garrison library." He recorded that it was an idea "that every officer has entered into."

Accordingly, he appropriated £1,000 from the fund and raised another £400 through subscriptions. He later reported that £500 had been spent on "books of character and value" from England as well as £100 on "others of light reading and trifling value" from New York. In order to import books from the United States a permit was required—from himself as lieutenant-governor.

The Officers' Garrison Library was established and eventually became today's Cambridge Military Library in Royal Artillery Park. When the British left Halifax in 1906, the library was transferred to Canada, along with the Citadel and other Imperial military and naval property. In 1934, with suitable fanfare, Lieutenant-Governor Walter Covert unveiled a plaque honouring Dalhousie's part in founding the library. Invitations to the ceremony were sent to several residents of Castine and Machias, but understandably perhaps, none of them chose to attend.

In this way, two of Halifax's oldest institutions, both devoted to education and broadening the mind, were founded from the spoils of war. New Brunswick, at whose new "border" these monies had been collected and at whose instigation the expedition had been mounted, received nothing.

The War of 1812 did not turn out as the United States expected. She had essentially gone to war because of Britain's policies on the high seas; in particular the Orders-in-Council, the impressment of American seamen, the violation of American territorial waters and the blockade of her ports. She sent her armies to invade Upper and Lower Canada at the time and place of her choosing, while Britain was heavily engaged in a bitter conflict with Napoleon.

Although the Americans won some naval victories on the Great Lakes, after two and a half years of fighting, the numerous attempts at invading Canada ended in failure. At sea, there had been a string of outstanding successes against the Royal Navy, but it was abruptly and unexpectedly broken by *Shannon*. The Americans had gambled and lost. Not one of the stated aims for which the United States originally went to war was achieved.

The Treaty of Ghent, signed in the Belgian city on Christmas Eve, 1814, essentially restored conditions to their prewar status in circumstances very favourable to the United States. Although the Americans were far more successful at the bargaining table than on the battlefield, 30 months of fighting on land and at sea, hundreds of deaths and injuries, the equivalent of millions of American dollars and British pounds of public and private property damage, as well as all the other expenses associated with war, had been for nothing in the end.

If the United States and Great Britain had only been the half-hearted enemies that Nova Scotia and New England were, it would not have been necessary to go to war at all.

BIBLIOGRAPHY

Abucar, Dr. Mohamed. *Struggle for Development: The Black Communities of North & East Preston and Cherry Brook, Nova Scotia 1784–1987*. Dartmouth: Black Cultural Centre, 1988.

Adams, Henry. *The War of 1812*. Washington, D.C.: The Infantry Journal, 1944.

Akins, Thomas Beamish. "The History of Halifax City," *Collections of the Nova Scotia Historical Society*, Vol. VIII, 1895 (2002 reprint).

Berton, Pierre. *Flames Across the Border 1813–1814*. Toronto: McClelland & Stewart, 1981.

Boileau, John. "Internees, Evacuees, and Immigrants." *The Beaver*. Vol. 84, No.1 (February/March 2004) 31–35.

Borrett, William Coates. *Historic Halifax in Tales Told Under the Old Town Clock*. Toronto: Ryerson, 1948.

Burt, A.L. *The United States, Great Britain and British North America from the Revolution to the Establishment of Peace after the War of 1812*. New York: Russell & Russell, 1961.

Chapman, Harry J. "The Battle of Hampden." *Sprague's Journal of Maine History*, Vol. 2, No. 4 (October 1914), 185–93.

Chidsey, Donald Barr. *The American Privateers*. New York: Dodd,

Mead & Company, 1962.

Clark, Rev. George F. "Military Operations at Castine, Maine." A
    Paper read before the Worcester Society of Antiquity,
    Worcester, February 5, 1889.

Copp, Walter Ronald. "Nova Scotian Trade during the War of
    1812." *The Canadian Historical Review.* Vol. 17 (1937),
    141–55.

———. "Military Activities in Nova Scotia during the War of
    1812." *Collections of the Nova Scotia Historical Society.* Vol.
    XXIV (1938), 57–74.

Cuthbertson, Brian. "Burials on Deadman's Island Northwest Arm:
    A Report Prepared for the Halifax Regional Municipality." June
    1998.

———. "Melville Island Prison During the War of 1812." *Journal
    of the Royal Nova Scotia Historical Society.* Vol. 6 (2003),
    40–64.

Deveau, J. Alphonse ed. and trans. *Diary of a Frenchman: François
    Lambert Bourneuf's Adventures from France to Acadia
    1787–1871.* Halifax: Nimbus, 1990.

Dupuy, R. Ernest and Trevor N. *The Collins Encyclopedia of
    Military History: From 3500 BC to the Present.* Chatham:
    BCA, 1993.

Elting, Col. John R. *Amateurs, To Arms!: A Military History of the
    War of 1812.* Chapel Hill: Algonquin, 1991.

Engelman, Fred L. *The Peace of Christmas Eve.* New York:
    Harcourt, Brace & World, 1962.

Evans, Dorothy Bezanson. *Hammonds Plains: The First 100 Years.*
    Halifax: Bounty, 1993.

Falkner, Leonard. For Jefferson and Liberty: *The United States in
    War and Peace, 1800–1815.* New York: Alfred A. Knopf, 1972.

Fergusson, C.B., ed. *A Documentary Study of the Establishment of
    the Negroes in Nova Scotia between the War of 1812 and the
    Winning of Responsible Government.* PANS Publication No.
    8. Halifax: Public Archives of Nova Scotia, 1948.

Forester, C.S. *The Age of Fighting Sail: The Story of the Naval War
    of 1812.* Garden City, N.Y.: Doubleday, 1956.

Gleig, G.R. *The Campaigns of the British Army at Washington and New Orleans in the Years 1814–1815*. 4th ed., London: John Murray, 1836.

Grant, Dr. John N. *The Immigration and Settlement of the Black Refugees of the War of 1812 in Nova Scotia and New Brunswick*. Dartmouth: Black Cultural Centre, 1990.

Grant, Kay. *Samuel Cunard: Pioneer of the Atlantic Steamship*. New York: Abelard-Schuman, 1967.

Gywnn, Julian. *Frigates and Foremasts: The North American Squadron in Nova Scotia Waters, 1745–1815*. Vancouver: University of British Columbia Press, 2003.

Haliburton, Thomas C. *History of Nova Scotia in Two Volumes*, Vol. II. Halifax: Joseph Howe, 1829 (facsimile reprint, Belleville: Mika, 1973).

Hampden Historical Society. "A Brief Military History of Hampden," *History of the Town of Hampden, Maine*. Ellsworth: Ellsworth American, 1976, 16–24.

———. *Call to Arms Celebration, Re-enactment of the Battle of Hampden, August 22-23-24, 1980*.

Hannay, James. "The War of 1812." *Collections of the Nova Scotia Historical Society for the Years 1899 and 1900, Vol XI*. 1901.

Hitsman, J. Mackay. *The Incredible War of 1812: A Military History*. Toronto: University of Toronto Press, 1965.

Horsman, Reginald. *The War of 1812*. New York: Alfred A. Knopf, 1969.

Horwood, Harold & Ed Butts. *Bandits & Privateers: Canada in the Age of Gunpowder*. Toronto: Doubleday, 1987.

Kert, Faye Margaret. *Prize and Prejudice: Privateering and Naval Prize in Atlantic Canada in the War of 1812*. Research in Maritime History No.11. St. John's, Nfld: International Maritime Economic History Association, 1997.

Leefe, John. *The Atlantic Privateers: Their Story—1749–1815*. Halifax: Petheric, 1978.

Lewis, Michael. *A Social History of the Navy 1793–1815*. London: George Allen & Unwin, 1960.

Logan, Major H. Meredith. "Melville Island, The Military Prison of

Halifax." *The Annual Journal of the United Services Institute.*
Vol. VI (1933) 12–34.

Lohnes, Barry J. "British Naval Problems at Halifax during the War
of 1812." *Mariner's Mirror.* Vol. 59 (1973) 317–33.

Lord, Walter. *The Dawn's Early Light.* New York: W.W. Norton,
1972.

Major, Marjorie. "Melville Island." *Nova Scotia Historical
Quarterly.* Vol. IV, No. 3 (1974) 253–72.

Marsters, Roger. *Bold Privateers: Terror, Plunder and Profit on
Canada's Atlantic Coast.* Halifax: Formac, 2004.

Martell, J.S. "Military Settlements in Nova Scotia after the War of
1812." *Collections of the Nova Scotia Historical Society.* Vol.
24, 75–105.

Maycock, Ben. "The Privateer." *The Beaver.* Vol. 83, No. 3
(June/July 2003) 8–13.

Morris, Cmdre. Charles. *The Autobiography of Commodore
Morris.* N.p, n.d.

Murdoch, Beamish. *A History of Nova-Scotia or Acadie, Volume III.*
Halifax: James Barnes, 1867.

Pachai, Dr. Bridglal. *Beneath the Clouds of the Promised Land:
The Survival of Nova Scotia's Blacks Volume II: 1800–1989.*
Hantsport: Lancelot, 1990.

Padfield, Peter. *Broke and the Shannon.* London: Hodder &
Stoughton, 1968.

Palmer, Benjamin F. *The Diary of Benjamin F. Palmer,
Privateersman: While a prisoner on board English warships at
sea, in the prison at Melville Island and at Dartmoor.* Acorn
Club, 1915.

Parker, Mike. *Fortress Halifax: Portrait of a Garrison Town.* Halifax:
Nimbus, 2004.

Poolman, Kenneth. *Guns Off Cape Ann: The Story of the Shannon
and the Chesapeake.* London: Evans Brothers, 1961.

Pullen, RAdm. H.F. *The Shannon and the Chesapeake.* Toronto:
McClelland & Stewart, 1970.

Raddall, Thomas H. *The Path of Destiny, Canada from the British
Conquest to Home Rule: 1763–1850.* Vol. III., Canadian

History Series. Toronto: Doubleday, 1957.

———. *Halifax: Warden of the North*. Halifax: Nimbus, 1993.

Regan, John W. *Sketches and Traditions of the Northwest Arm*. 3rd ed. Halifax: 1928.

Reilly, Robin. *The British at the Gates: The New Orleans Campaign in the War of 1812*. New York: G.P. Putnam's Sons, 1974.

Snider, C.H.J. *Under the Red Jack: Privateers of the Maritime Provinces of Canada in the War of 1812*. Toronto: Musson, 1928.

Stanley, George F.G. "British Operations on the Penobscot in 1814." *Journal of the Society for Army Historical Research*. Vol. XIX, No. 75 (Autumn 1940) 168–78.

———. *The War of 1812: Land Operations*. Toronto: Macmillan, 1983.

Tully, Andrew. *When They Burned the White House*. New York: Simon & Schuster, 1961.

Waterhouse, Benjamin, (pseudonym of Dr. Amos Babcock) ed. *A Journal of a Young Man of Massachusetts, Late a Surgeon on Board an American Privateer, who was Captured at Sea by the British, in May Eighteen Hundred and Thirteen, and was Confined First, at Melville Island, Halifax, then at Chatham, in England, and last, at Dartmoor Prison. Interspersed with Observations, Anecdotes and Remarks, Tending to Illustrate the Moral and Political Characters of Three Nations, to which is Added, a Correct Engraving of Dartmoor Prison, Representing the Massacre of American Prisoners. Written by Himself*. Boston: Rowe & Hooper, 1816.

Watts, Heather & Michèle Raymond. *Halifax's Northwest Arm: An Illustrated History*. Halifax: Formac, 2003.

Webster, Donald B. "The Penobscot Expedition of 1814." *Tradition*. Vol. IV, No. 1 (January 1961) 45–57.

Whitfield, Harvey Amani. "Black Refugee Communities in Early Nineteenth Century Nova Scotia." *Journal of the Royal Nova Scotia Historical Society*. Vol. 6 (2003) 92–109.

Williamson, William D. *The History of the State of Maine from its First Discovery, A.D. 1602, to the Separation, A.D. 1820,*

Inclusive. Vol. II. Hallowell: Glazier, Masters, 1832 (facsimile reprint, Freeport: Cumberland, n.d.).

———. "British Officers on the Penobscot, in 1814." *Bangor Historical Magazine.* n.d., p. 27.

Winks, Robin W. *The Blacks in Canada: A History.* Montreal: McGill-Queen's University Press, 1972.

Wood, William, ed. *Select British Documents of the Canadian War of 1812, Volume III, Part I.* Toronto: The Champlain Society, 1926.

———. *Select British Documents of the Canadian War of 1812, Volume III, Part II.* Toronto: The Champlain Society, 1928.

ILLUSTRATION CREDITS AND SOURCES

Page 20, map edited and altered by Peggy McCalla; pp. 22, 33, 114, Horsman, Reginald. *War of 1812*, Eyre & Spottiswoode, 1969; pp. 43, 45, Poolman, Kenneth. *Guns off Cape Ann*, Evans brothers, 1961; pp. 52, 59, 60, Marsters, Roger. *Bold Privateers: Terror Plunder and Profit on Canada's Atlantic Coast*, Formac, 2004; p. 75, Deveau, J. Alphonse. *Diary of a Frenchman*, Nimbus, 1990; p. 81, Watts, Heather and Raymond, Michèle. *Halifax's Northwest Arm*, Formac, 2003; p. 86, John Boileau; pp. 100, 103, 120, Lord, Walter. *The Dawn's Early Light*, W.W. Norton & Co., 1972; pp.106, 162, Stanley, George. *The War of 1812: Land Operations*, Macmillan, 1983; p.164, Fingard, Judith, Guildford, Janet, Sutherland, David. *Halifax The First 250 Years*, Formac, 1999; back cover author photograph, Mark Doucette.

INDEX